LEVEL 3

Text Production & Word Processing

Jill Dowson

Endorsed by OCR for the Certificates in Text Processing

www.heinemann.co.uk
✓ Free online support
✓ Useful weblinks
✓ 24 hour online ordering

01865 888058

Heinemann

Inspiring generations

Heinemann Educational Publishers
Halley Court, Jordan Hill, Oxford OX2 8EJ
Part of Harcourt Education

Heinemann is the registered trademark of
Harcourt Education Limited

Text © Jill Dowson, 2004

First published 2004

090807060504
10987654321

British Library Cataloguing in Publication Data is available from the British Library
on request.

ISBN 0 435 45368 8

Typeset by TechType, Abingdon, Oxon

Printed by Thomson Litho Ltd

Acknowledgements
I am grateful to Anna Fabrizio at Heinemann Educational for her support and
encouragement. I am also indebted to Alex Gray for his expertise and sound advice
that turns my cygnets into swans. Thank you to my colleagues at OCR for their
continued support.

The author and publisher would like to thank OCR Examinations Board for
permission to reproduce a past examination paper in this book.

Tel: 01865 888058 www.heinemann.co.uk

Contents

Introduction

This book is designed for you to build on the word processing skills you have acquired already in order to progress to more advanced work. Although a lot of revision notes are provided, it presumes that you have a basic knowledge of how to use Microsoft Word to produce documents at OCR Levels 1 and 2, as covered in the previous student book.

This book contains the background information and practice exercises you require to prepare for the OCR Text Processing exam units in

- Text Production Level 3 (Advanced)
- Word Processing Level 3 (Advanced)

The book is divided into four sections:

Section 1 – Basic knowledge and skills

This provides notes on health and safety and revision of basic rules and conventions necessary for producing the documents required for the text processing unit exams. It gives detailed information and hints, together with exercises.

Section 2 – Text production

This provides detailed information and hints, together with exercises for you to practise the skills you need to master before attempting a full practice exam for this unit.

Section 3 – Word processing

This provides detailed information and hints, together with exercises and recall text for you to practise the skills you need to master before attempting a full practice exam for this unit.

Section 4 – Exam work

This provides a sample OCR word processing exam with incorrectly worked documents to illustrate common errors and how to avoid them. It is followed by two new practice exams similar to OCR standard for each unit, together with recall text.

Section 5 – Worked examples

This provides worked examples of each of the exercises and practice exams given in Sections 1–4, for you to check against your own work.

Section 6 – Letterheads and memo headings

This provides printed headed paper, should you prefer to use it, for all the exercises and practice exams in Sections 1–4.

CD-ROM

Inside the front cover of this book is a CD-ROM that contains the following:

- Recall text for you to insert in your files for the word processing exercises and practice exams.
- Headings for you to recall as templates when working on letter and memo documents.

More about OCR exams and Heinemann textbooks

The two exams in this book are units from the OCR Level 3 Certificate in Text Processing. In the Heinemann Skills series there is a tutor resource file to support these units. OCR also offers exams in text processing units at Levels 1 and 2, and there are student books and tutor resource files to support some of these.

Each exam unit is a worthwhile achievement in its own right, but you can gain the full OCR Level 3 Certificate in Text Processing by passing:

- Text Production Level 3 (Advanced) – core unit.
- Word Processing Level 3 (Advanced) – optional unit.

You might then like to work towards the Diploma, which can be gained by passing the core unit and three optional units of your choice. You can add on as many extra optional units as you like. Your tutor or OCR centre can give you details.

Section 1

Basic knowledge and skills

This section covers:

* Notes on personal health and safety when using computers
* Revision notes on proofreading, spellcheck and grammar check
* Information about paper and font styles and sizes
* Revision notes on basic rules and conventions for business documents
* OCR spelling, abbreviation and correction sign lists
* Revision exercises on some of these aspects

Health and safety

If you follow these guidelines, you will be able to work at your computer safely and comfortably:

* Avoid trailing flexes and clutter.
* Avoid eating or drinking while working at your computer.
* Know where the master switch is to turn off electrical equipment quickly in an emergency.
* Familiarise yourself with the fire drill for the building you are in.

Personal safety

It is important to avoid eyestrain and repetitive strain injury when operating a computer. Correct posture can help to prevent these. Sit straight in front of your keyboard and screen. Adjust your chair so that the middle of the computer screen is in line with your eyes. Your copyholder should be close to the left or right of your screen and at a similar height. Your mouse should be to the side of and on the same level as your keyboard.

Posture checklist
* **Head** – hold erect with chin slightly tucked in.
* **Shoulders** – avoid hunching, hold them back but relaxed.
* **Body** – centre yourself opposite the space bar and a hand's length away from the keyboard.
* **Back** – keep straight, with your body sloping slightly forward from the hips and the chair back supporting your waist.
* **Arms** – let them hang loosely with elbows tucked into your sides.
* **Wrists** – keep them level and avoid dropping or arching them.
* **Hands** – keep close together and level across the backs.
* **Fingers** – curve and rest them lightly on or hovering just above the keys.
* **Feet** – rest both feet flat on the floor.

Practise so that you become comfortable and relaxed in this position.

Taking a break

Avoid working on your computer for long periods without a break. Collecting work from the printer, proofreading printouts or distributing work can provide a useful break from the tension of operating a computer.

Stress-busting exercises

The following exercises can be done from a sitting position and whilst remaining at the computer desk, although you will need to push yourself back a little to allow for arm movements.

ALL MOVEMENTS NEED TO BE DONE SLOWLY AND DELIBERATELY

Sit up straight, with arms hanging down and hands relaxed. Legs should be slightly apart, with both feet on the floor. Keep chin slightly tucked in. Then

- shrug shoulders strongly up towards ears, hold and then release – 4 times
- squeeze shoulder blades together, hold and then release – 4 times
- rotate shoulders slowly – 4 times forwards, 4 times backwards, then relax
- keeping shoulders straight:
  tilt head slowly from side to side – 4 times
  nod head slowly up and down – 4 times
  look over right/left shoulder – 4 times each side
- holding arms out straight in front, make fists and flex wrists up and down then round and round several times, then relax
- flex fingers (as if casting a spell), shake hands vigorously and rub them together.

You can use any of these exercises if your muscles are feeling tense, although you may not always have the time or feel the need to work through the complete routine. The exercises can also be used on a cold day for warming up prior to keyboarding.

Proofreading, spellcheck and grammar check

Proofreading

In your work at Levels 1 and 2, you will have realised that efficient proofreading is the key to producing accurate copy. In the exams, candidates incur more penalties through failing to spot their own keying-in errors than for any other reason. In the Text Production Level 3 exam you are required to identify and correct errors. **They are not circled at this level.** The type of errors you will have to identify are:

- **Typographical (keying in mistakes)** – p;lease, cam4e, andd, befroe, no space between words.
- **Spelling** – acommodation, recieved.
- **Agreement (mistakes in grammar)** – he are here, find 6 error.
- **Punctuation** – omitted full stop, no initial capital starting a sentence, missing/ misplaced apostrophe.

Spellcheck and alternative spellings

Use the spellchecking facility as a first line check, but you should not rely upon it as a substitute for careful proofreading. It will not always identify errors if they are still recognisable words or occur in names or technical terms, nor will it highlight omitted, additional or substituted words.

OCR will only accept the English spelling of words in its exams. American spellings such as *center* and *color* are not allowed. Check that you have the correct default setting for spelling and grammar options by using **Tools** → **Language** → **Set Language** → select **English (United Kingdom)** → click **Default** and **OK**. Alternative English spellings are acceptable as long as they are spelt the same throughout the document, eg adviser/advisor, despatch/dispatch, organise/organize, spelt/spelled.

Grammar check

This can be a useful facility in identifying some of the basic errors, but it can be confusing as it sometimes highlights portions of text which are accepted as the correct use of English. When in doubt, read the text carefully to make sure it makes sense and check it carefully against the original copy.

Abbreviation and spelling lists

The following lists contain the words which OCR uses to test spellings and abbreviations in the Text Production Level 3 exam. **Remember, they are not circled at this level.** Learning the correct spellings and expansions of these words before you sit the exam will give you confidence and help you to avoid penalties.

Abbreviations

You will need to recognise and correctly expand the following abbreviations, which may be used. You may use dictionaries and spellcheckers in any of the OCR modular exams.

a/c(s)	account(s)	necy	necessary
appt(s)	appointment(s)	opp(s)	opportunity/ies
approx	approximate(ly)	org	organisation
cat(s)	catalogue(s)	poss	possible
co(s)	company/ies	ref(s)	reference(s)
dept(s)	department(s)	ref(d)	refer(red)
dr	dear	sec(s)	secretary/ies
gntee(s)	guarantee(s)	temp	temporary
immed	immediate(ly)	sig(s)	signature(s)
info	information	yr(s)	year(s)
mfr(s)	manufacturer(s)	yr(s)	your(s)
misc	miscellaneous		

days of the week, eg	Wed, Sat	months of the year, eg **Feb, Nov**			
parts of addresses, eg	Ave Avenue	Pk Park		Sq Square	

Cres	Crescent	**Pl**	Place	**St**	Street
Dr	Drive	**Rd**	Road		

complimentary closes, eg **Yrs ffly** Yours faithfully **Yrs sncly** Yours sincerely

Where an abbreviation has more than one expansion you will need to read the text carefully and choose the one which makes sense.

Spelling

You will need to correct the spelling of words taken from the following list. This includes possible derivations of these words (eg plurals, -ed, -ing, -ment, -tion, -ly, -able, -ible).

access	colleague	permanent
accommodate	committee	receipt
achieve	correspondence	receive
acknowledge	definite	recommend
advertisement	develop	responsible
although	discuss	satisfactory
apparent	expense	separate
appreciate	experience	success
believe	financial	sufficient
business	foreign	temporary
cancel	government	through
client	inconvenient	unfortunate

The following exercise is designed to test your proofreading skills.

Exercise 1.1

Identify the errors and key in a corrected copy of the text, expanding any abbreviations. Print a copy of your work and check it with the worked example on page 108.

> Our exciting new cat is now out. Chose form british hotel stays to foregn tours. Our co inspectors checks catering and accomodation to ensure it is of the high standard hour customers demand.
>
> we reccomend our star value holidays with ful board, excursions and activities all icluded in the price. We can gntee that you will recieve value for money. We also offers a selection off special interest holidays, each hosted buy an experianced tutors.

Paper and font styles and sizes

Paper

In the exams all documents should be produced on A4 paper. Single sheets of A4 or continuous computer sheets are accepted. Letters must be printed on headed A4 and memos must include *TO/FROM* headings, otherwise you will incur penalties. Any continuation pages must be on plain paper.

Letterhead and memo headings may be of any design and can be prepared as templates for you to recall into your files, or you can key in your own design at the start of the document. Copies of letterheads used throughout this book can be found on the CD-ROM.

The paper sizes commonly used in business are:

- A3 – 297 mm x 420 mm
- A4 – 210 mm x 297 mm
- A5 – 148 mm x 210 mm
- A6 – 105 mm x 148 mm

When the shorter edge is at the top, this is known as **portrait** style. Most business documents, and invariably correspondence, are presented in this way. When the longer edge is at the top, this is known as **landscape** style. Documents such as tables, databases and spreadsheets are often presented in this way.

In the Word Processing Level 3 exam you will be required to format the tabulation document in landscape style. Instructions on how to do this are given in Section 3.

Font

For exam purposes a plain, easily read font such as Times New Roman, Arial or Courier is preferred. The pitch size for normal text should be 10 to 12. Examiners may find it difficult to mark scripts printed in a smaller pitch.

Times New Roman and Arial are **proportionally spaced**, giving each character an amount of space appropriate to the character width. Courier has **monospaced** font, with each character having the same width. All the fonts shown here are in 12 pitch. Compare the following.

will	little	offer	Times New Roman
will	little	offer	Arial
will	little	offer	Courier
will	little	offer	OpenHand

It can be fun to explore the different font styles and pitch sizes and discover which are most suited to various tasks and which are the easiest, or most difficult, to read. You might like to do this when practising suitable drills or exercises in this book.

Punctuation marks

Style

Open punctuation means only using it where essential grammatically or to clarify meaning. **Full punctuation** means using it throughout a document, including abbreviations, dates and addresses. Although full punctuation is rarely used nowadays, both styles are acceptable in OCR exams.

At this level, you will already have chosen your preferred style and mastered its basic rules. However, you may find a little revision helpful, covering a couple of the more complex aspects.

Brackets and **quotation marks** should be keyed in without spacing between the brackets or quotes and the adjacent words within them, eg

'We absolutely adored "Switchback" at the Stag Theatre', enthused Lucy and her mother (Mrs Worthington).

In the exam, you should follow copy regarding single or double quotes. Check your work carefully, as you could incur two penalties (one for each word) if you omit a set of brackets or quotes.

Dashes are used to separate words, so there should be spaces either side, eg

A busy Mum – single with two toddlers – you won't have much time to yourself.

A dash can also be used as a substitute for *to*, when it is acceptable with or without spaces. All of the following styles are correct:

1300 – 1330 hrs   Monday – Friday   2003–4   pages 19–30

Hyphens are used to link words, so there should not be spaces within the words, eg

Keep in touch by e-mail, as we need to review this on a day-to-day basis.

The **solidus** (oblique or forward slash) should not have a space to either side of it. It should not be confused with the back slash, which is not acceptable as an alternative. In these exams the solidus is used in references.

FO/PR   Festival/music/2004   va/asu/moderate/mlet/premod1

Apostrophes

Text Production Level 3 tests your knowledge of the correct use of apostrophes. You have to identify and correct misplaced, omitted or superfluous apostrophes. Many candidates find this difficult and incur penalties, so it is worth spending a little time on revising the basic rules.

Apostrophes are used to indicate possession:

In the singular an **apostrophe** and s are added, as in

>   A student's mobile phone – the mobile phone belonging to a student
>   A college's phone number – the phone number of a college

In the plural (when the word ends in s or es) an **apostrophe** is added, as in

>   The students' mobile phones – the mobile phones belonging to several students
>   The colleges' phone numbers – the phone numbers of several colleges

In the plural (when the word does not end in s) an **apostrophe** and s are added, as in

>   The workmen's instructions – the instructions of several workmen
>   The people's stadium – the stadium belonging to many people

Apostrophes are also used to indicate omission of letters:

>   he'll (he will)   they'd (they would) aren't (are not)   I've (I have)
>   that's (that is)   hadn't (had not)   you're (you are)   I'm (I am)

Only use an apostrophe in **it's** for *it is*, otherwise use **its** for *belonging to it.*

Only use an apostrophe in **you're** for *you are*, otherwise use **your** for *belonging to you.*

Only use an apostrophe in **there's** for *there is*, otherwise use **theirs** for *belonging to them.*

The following exercise will give you extra practice with these rules.

Exercise 1.2

Key in the following sentences, correcting the errors in the use of apostrophes. Some are misplaced, some are missing and others have been added where they are not needed. Print a copy of your work and check it with the worked example on page 109.

> The passengers' in the back seat were alarmed as the cars' speed increased.
>
> I leave college in two week's time. Its amazing how time flies!
>
> The hotels jacuzzi accommodates' 10. Each seat has it's own control to alter the jet flow.
>
> This companys' director is also on two associated companie's boards', but its all above board!
>
> The childrens' toys are displayed in the stores' window. The ladie's wear is located on the first floor.

Capitals

In the exams *you are expected to follow copy*, otherwise you may incur penalties. However, you are allowed to substitute initial capitals in appropriate instances, eg

- in a table or list, where the first letter of each item in a column is drafted in lower case (MS Word will usually alter such letters to capitals automatically)
- in job titles, where *head of department* is acceptable as *Head of Department*.

If you choose to alter such capitalisation, you must be consistent throughout the document. Words in full capitals, such as headings, should only be altered if following an editing instruction. **The best tip is to follow the exam draft.**

A reminder of the basic rules:

- Sentences always start with capital letters. This is tested in the text production exam.
- Always use a capital *I* when it stands for you, eg 'I'm on my own'. 'Here I go again!' 'I love you'.
- Use initial capitals for proper nouns, eg 'I'll lend you *Danger Lurks* by Elliot Hodge. He's a Detective Inspector, so he knows his subject. It will make ideal holiday reading when you go to Allicante in July.'
- Use capitals at the beginning of quoted speech, 'Emily complained "I can't find what I want in the sales", and then suggested "Let's spend the money on a meal out instead".'
- **Do not** use initial capitals for seasons, eg 'The autumns and winters are becoming warmer but wetter.'

Figures and symbols

In the exams *you are expected to follow copy*, as style of figures, symbols and choice of words or figures are drafted correctly. Calculations and statistics are not tested in these exams.

Numerals versus words

Numbers are usually expressed as numerals

* in descriptive text – numbers above 10
* in dates and times
* in precise quantities, weights and measures
* for calculations and statistics – $\sqrt{16}$, $6\overline{)39}$
* for identification – 3 High Street, M4, pages 5–9.

Commas or spaces may be used within large numbers – 1,500 or 1 500, 11,500,000 or 11 500 000.

Numbers are usually expressed as words

* in descriptive text – numbers below 10
* in imprecise quantities – two or three occasions, thousands of plants
* in titles and names – Ten-Acre Farm, the Hundred-Years' War

and *always* when

* starting a sentence
* not being used as an amount – 'It's one of those days, as one grows older, It's one or other.'

Style

The chosen style of display should be used consistently throughout the document.

Abbreviations
* A space may be left between the figure and abbreviation or it may be keyed close up – 100 % or 100%　2 kg or 2kg　1.5 cm or 1.5cm　0900 hrs or 0900hrs 15 mm × 20 mm or 15mm × 20mm (here a space is needed either side of the ×).
* Symbols may be substituted for words – 　for euro, ℓ for litre.

Times
* Either the 24-hour or 12-hour clock may be used – 1430 hrs/hours or 2.30 pm.
* There is *no point* required in the 24-hour clock.

Money
* No space should be left between the money symbol and the sum.
* Sums of money may contain commas or spaces – £19,000 or £19 000 500,100,000 or　500 100 000　$750,000 or $750 000
* In columns, units should be aligned and decimal points aligned under each other. **In columns with totals this style of display is vital.**

Decimals

- Numbers of less than one unit need a zero in front of the decimal point – 0.2, 0.65.
- In lists or tables, whole amounts may be displayed with zeros and decimal points. This makes alignment easier, improves appearance and is easier to read –

£15.99	18.25 ℓ
£00.95	15.00 ℓ
£30.00	02.05 ℓ

Note: Elsewhere in Europe, a comma is commonly used as the decimal marker.

Fractions

- Common fractions such as $^1/_2$, $^3/_4$, $^5/_8$ are accessed in MS Word by **Insert** → **Symbol** → select **Font** → click on the fraction from the grid → **Insert**.
- There should be no space between any whole number and such fraction – $6^7/_8$, $5^1/_4$, $1^1/_2$.
- If the required fractions are not available in symbols, they can be keyed as 11/12 or 1/30 but there must be a space between any whole number and such fraction – 8 3/10.
- In continuous text simple fractions should be spelled out – 'The journey from home to the coast takes about three-quarters of an hour.'

The following exercise will help you to revise some of these rules.

Exercise 1.3

Key in the text below, making amendments to ensure correct and consistent style. Correct the apostrophe errors. Print a copy of your work and check it with the worked example on page 110.

Run-Master Folding Treadmill

This updated treadmill features the 'Easy Fold" system, which allows it to be folded to ½ it's size with minimal effort. The console offers 7 programmes, including heart rate control. Pulse rate monitoring is carried out via a wireless chest belt (included in the accessories) .

The equipment is fully guaranteed with a lifetime cover on the frame and 10 year's cover on the motor. The treadmill weighs 91 kg and part of it needs assembling. There is a large LED display showing time, speed, distance and incline. It also calculates heart rate and calories used. There are three target, 3 pre- set and 2 heart rate control programmes.

The powered elevation range is 0 % to 15 per cent. The running surface is 132 cm x 45cm and overall dimensions are 163 cm x91 cm x 145cm. The equipment is designed to be used by persons weighing no more than 120kg (265lb). The price for the complete package is £ 995.

Page breaks

You will have learned that although MS word automatically makes its own *soft page breaks*, you can alter these by holding down **Control** and pressing **Enter** to insert a *hard page break*. Soft page breaks are moved automatically when changes are made to a document during editing. Hard page breaks are not moved during editing, as the software always reads them as a command to start a new page, no matter where they appear.

In one document of the word processing exam you are required to remove existing hard page breaks and insert your own. This can easily be done by deleting the **Page Break** instruction that is revealed when the ¶ (**Show/Hide**) icon is clicked.

In other documents in the text production and word processing exams, you may make your own page breaks, but you should ensure that at least two lines of text are left at the bottom of the first page and at least two lines are carried forward to the second page. Leaving the complimentary close of a letter as the only text on a continuation page should be avoided. The page break should be made so that at least two lines of a paragraph appear above the complimentary close.

Continuous text does not have to be split over two pages at a full stop. It is often better not to do so, as it can lead to confusion as to whether a new paragraph has been started at that point.

Another pitfall to be avoided is separating a heading from its relevant text. It is better to have a wide bottom margin than to split a heading from its following paragraph, list or table.

Paragraphs, margins, linespacing and headings

Style

In OCR text processing exams paragraphs are drafted in blocked style, ie each line of text starting at the left margin, with a ragged right margin. Although equal margins are most effective when displaying a document, the style of headed paper may dictate the size of the margins. A minimum of 1.3 cm is acceptable in the exams, but 2.5 cm is preferred.

It is useful to remind yourself of the default settings for margins, which are:

Top and Bottom 2.45 cm   Left and Right   3.17 cm

By this stage you will have learned how to set your own margins. In the exams you may set your own or use the default margins (pre-set by MS Word), or use fully justified margins (blocked to the left and right), except where instructed to do otherwise. You may sometimes wish to alter the margins. You may need to fit another line of text onto the page or make sure that a footnote stays with its related text. Of course, *in continuous text the left margin must always be aligned.*

Linespacing and headings

You will be familiar with keying text in single and double linespacing. This is a reminder of the basic rules.

- Text in single linespacing should have one clear linespace consistently between paragraphs.
- Text in double linespacing may have similar spacing but often needs *extra* linespacing to indicate the start of each paragraph clearly.
- There should be at least one clear linespace before and after headings.

In the exams, penalties will be incurred for inconsistent linespacing within a document or where the start of each new paragraph is not obvious.

You should follow draft regarding capitalisation and underlining. However, in addition, you may embolden, underline or centre headings as long as similar headings are consistent throughout the document.

Centring and display

Some form of display, including centring, underlining, emboldening, capitalisation and altering font size or style is required in the exams. You will already be familiar with the following methods, but it is useful to remind yourself of the rules for exam purposes.

Centring

You will be required to centre text as you key it in and centre text that has been recalled. It should be centred over the text line (not necessarily the width of the page).

Underlining

You should follow draft in the exam and will incur a penalty for omitted underlining. The underline may include following punctuation but should not include the space either side of a single word or phrase. Additional underlining of headings is accepted.

Capitalisation

It is important to follow the draft carefully, as many penalties can be incurred through not doing so. At Level 3 you will be required to change the capitalisation of a section of text. To avoid re-keying and any resulting errors, mark the text to be altered, then use the **Format** → **Change Case** facility or **Shift+F3**. Use of capitals as a form of emphasis is acceptable.

Font style and size

This can be a very effective method of emphasising text. In Word Processing Level 3 you are required to change the font style and/or size of a section of text. Once you have marked the relevant text, use **Format** → **Font** and click on the font, style and size you want. This method allows you to see the effect in the preview box. Alternatively you can use the font boxes on the left of the formatting toolbar. Bear in mind that the chosen format needs to be easily read by the examiner.

Linespacing and insetting

Another acceptable method of emphasising a section of text is to alter the linespacing or inset it. In Word Processing Level 3 candidates are asked to inset a portion of text from both left and right margins. To be certain that you inset text by exactly the right amount, mark your text, use **Format** → **Paragraph** → **Indents and Spacing** → **Indentation Left** or **Right** select the measurement(s) you need → **OK**.

Lists and columns

You will already have learned about displaying and sorting lists. In Text Production Level 3 you are required to rearrange numbered lists and in Word Processing Level 3 you are instructed to sort a list into alphabetical, numerical or chronological (date) order. Remember that listed items should always be aligned and have the same linespacing between them.

Columns

In Word Processing Level 3 you are required to produce a two-column, newspaper style article. You may not have met this before. It is not difficult and detailed instructions and hints are given in Section 3 of this book.

Correction signs

You will have already met most of the correction signs used in the OCR exams. In Text Production Level 3 there are a couple of extra signs which you may not be familiar with. You may find the following list useful whilst you are learning the signs.

CORRECTION SIGNS USED IN TEXT PRODUCTION AND WORD PROCESSING
EXAMS AT LEVEL 3

You will need to recognise the following signs and what they mean in order to
amend text as drafted in the exams.

 **New paragraph** – start a new paragraph from
this point onwards

Run on – ignore the paragraph break and
continue typing on the same line

 **Insertion** – insert the words at the point of the
sign

 **Horizontal transposition** – switch the words so
that the first section comes after the second

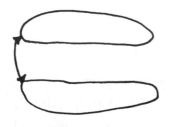 **Vertical transposition** – switch the circled
sections of text so that they change places as
shown by the arrows

... with ✓ in the margin   **Stet** – retain only the word/s with the line of
dashes underneath

/   **Space** – leave one space at this point

Close up – remove the extra space here

Align – move to the right

Align – move to the left

Section 2

Text production

This exam may be word processed or typewritten and must be completed within 1¼ hours. You have to produce three documents – a letter, a memo and a report or article.

Your work must contain no more than 17 faults overall to achieve a pass and no more than 6 faults overall to gain a distinction. Practice exams are provided in Section 4.

In this section you will practise the following skills, which are tested in the exam:

- Using letterheading and laying out a business letter
- Using memo heading and laying out a memo
- Altering linespacing
- Insetting text from left margin
- Emphasising, underlining and centring text
- Inserting and deleting text
- Rearranging numbered items
- Interpreting amendment and correction signs (given in Section 1)
- Expanding abbreviations from the OCR list (given in Section 1)
- Identifying and correcting the spelling of words from OCR list (given in Section 1)
- Identifying and correcting typographical and grammatical errors
- Identifying and correcting punctuation errors
- Selecting and inserting information from another document and from dictated material
- Postdating a document
- Indicating single and multiple enclosures
- Inserting footnotes and page numbers

Business letters

Layout and style

Any style of headed paper may be used, either by recalling a template (samples are provided on the CD-ROM) or by printing on to a pre-printed letterhead (samples given in Section 6). The font chosen should be easily read. Times New Roman or Arial in 10 to 12 pitch are popular with examiners.

It is worth reminding yourself of the layout and requirements for a business letter in the exams. At this level, the name, address and reference details, together with the subject heading, are shown in the rubric at the start of the document. **No indication is given as to layout and it is up to you to use an acceptable form of display.**

The example shown here is in fully blocked style (each line starts at the left margin), with open punctuation. This is the style used in OCR text processing exams. At least one clear linespace should be left between each separate item, with equal spacing between paragraphs.

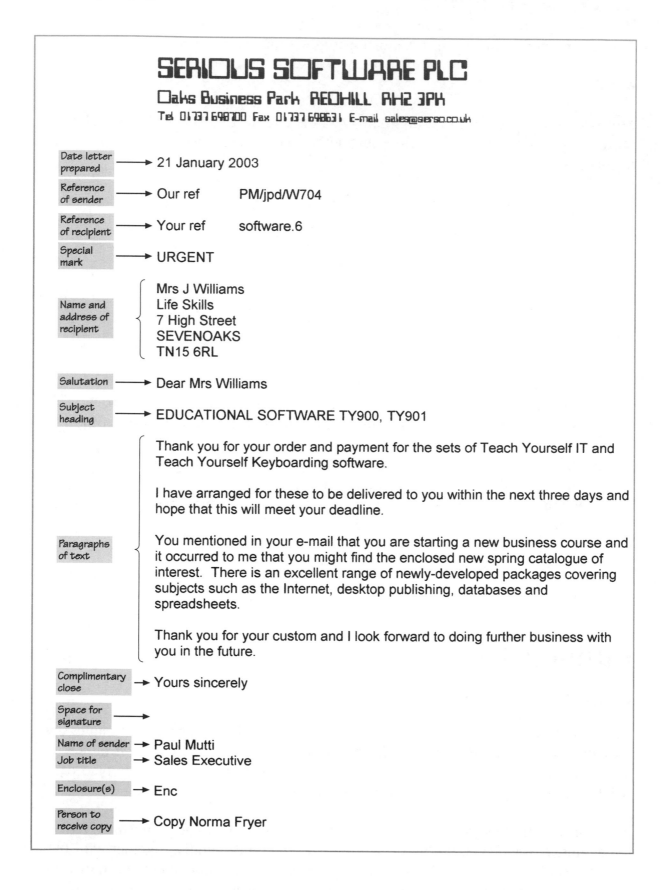

Date

You are required to date each letter with the date on which you are taking the exam. It is important that you do this, otherwise you will lose 3 marks. No instruction will be given in the draft but a reminder is given on the front cover of the question paper. A good position for the date is before or after the reference(s). MS Word will do this automatically if you use Insert → **Date and Time** *check Language box shows English (UK)* → select style from formats → **OK**.

The following styles are all acceptable:

10 March 2004   10th March 04   March 10 2004   10 Mar 04   10.3.04

The last example, all in figures, is more suitable for use in forms. When using all figures, if the month is shown before the day, ie 3.10.04, a penalty will be incurred as it could be read as 3 October 2004.

Reference

The words *Our ref* and *Your ref* may be displayed in any style but the reference must be keyed in *exactly* as shown in the draft, following spacing, punctuation and capitalisation. If no reference is shown in the draft one should not be added, as this will incur a penalty.

Special mark

In the Text Production Level 3 exam, you are instructed to key in a special mark on either the letter or memo. The special mark is used to signify special treatment of the document, eg *By Hand, Personal, Private and Confidential, Urgent.* Follow the capitalisation given in the draft. It is best placed immediately before the name and address of the recipient of a letter. In the workplace this makes it less likely to be omitted when addressing an envelope or label and it can be clearly seen through a window envelope.

Name and address

In the exam you should follow draft with regard to capitalisation, otherwise you will lose marks. If the recipient's first name is given in full, that is how it must be keyed in. Substituting an initial in that case would be penalised.

The name of the town should be in capitals with the name of the county in initial capitals. Abbreviations for *Drive, Street, Crescent,* etc. should be expanded but the county may remain abbreviated. The postcode should have one space between its two halves. It may appear on a separate line or on the same line as the town/county and separated from it by several spaces. When using open punctuation, there is no need to insert any punctuation within the address.

Mr Stephen Spencer
20 Marlborough Drive
BURLEY
Hants   BH24 6AD

Salutation and complimentary close

The salutation and complimentary close should match.

Dear Sir(s)/Madam . . . Yours faithfully   Dear Mr Singh . . . Yours sincerely

Try to leave at least five clear linespaces for the signature. If you leave different spacing, in an attempt to spread the letter out or to fit it on one page, that is accepted in the exam. Do not add a signature in the signature space, as this would be penalised.

Enclosure(s)

In the text production exam you are required to show whether the enclosure is single or multiple where the text states that one item or several items are enclosed, attached or included. All of the following forms are acceptable.

Enc/Encs enc/encs   ENC/ENCS   Att/Atts   ------- (in margin alongside
each mention in text)

Continuation sheet

If the letter goes on to a second page that page should be printed on plain paper. It should also be numbered, but no other details need appear (other than your name and centre number). At least two lines of text should be taken onto the continuation sheet along with the complimentary close. Do not number a single sheet document.

Correction of errors

In the exam, you need to identify and correct keying and punctuation errors as well as faulty spellings of words from the OCR list given in Section 1. **They are not circled at Level 3.**

Grammatical errors will only be tested in document 2. If the letter is drafted as the 2nd exam document, it will contain obvious errors of agreement, eg *he were* or *ten set of books* and less obvious ones, eg *The temp we brought in to cover the extra work are very efficient* or *The garden centre's display of trees and shrubs were magnificent.*

Correction signs

You must amend the text you key in according to the correction signs given in Section 1.

Abbreviations

Abbreviated words from the list given in Section 1 are included and you must expand these correctly.

Postdating

In the exam, usually in the letter or memo, you are instructed to provide a date for a precise day in the following month, eg

I will get in touch on Monday give date for first Monday of next month so that we can consider the plans in detail.

Worked Example: I will get in touch on Monday 1 September so that we can consider the plans in detail.

The correct date and month must be inserted, but the year is optional. Any one of the date styles previously shown is acceptable.

Internet and e-mail addresses

When keying in an e-mail or Internet address, your computer may change the colour of the text and underline it. This is accepted in the exam, but you may alter it if you prefer. To do this, mark the address then use **Format → Font →** select **Underline (none)** and **Colour (black)**. Be careful not to click on the hand icon when marking the text, otherwise your computer will start to connect you to the Internet.

The following exercises will give you extra practice in the above features before you attempt a full practice exam.

Exercise 2.1

Key in this exercise using a letterheading from the CD. Follow the layout shown in the book. Date with today's date, amend as shown, expanding the abbreviations and correcting a spelling and an apostrophe error. Print a copy and check it with the worked example on page 111.

Letter to Mrs L Mackie 63 Atlantic Quay GLASGOW G2 9KD
Our ref IB/Intro/id Please use the heading INTERNET ACCESS

Your ref   M72811

Dr Mrs Mackie

Our ~~free~~ Internet banking service makes life so much easier.

You can also pay bills and transfer money.

You can check your ~~recent~~ transactions and up-to-date balance immed, at the click of a mouse. This info is available at any time, day or night, for 365 days of the year.

There is no need to open any new a/cs. It is simply an alternative way of acessing your existing one's. Of course, you can still continue to contact us using traditional methods: by visiting a branch or telephoning.

We can assure you that our levels of security are of the ~~best~~ ~~highest~~. We provide an Internet banking fraud gntee. This ensures that, in the unlikely event of fraud, we will refund your money.

To register, go to www.centurybank.com/register and complete the short application form. Alternativly you can register at any of our branches.

We enclose a leaflet giving further details of this service, including contact numbers and e-mail addresses.

We look forward to hearing from you and welcoming you online soon.

Yrs sncly

Iain Duncan
Technology Manager

Exercise 2.2

Key in this exercise using a letterheading from the CD. Amend as shown and correct all word errors. Print a copy and check it with the worked example on page 112.

Letter to Mrs E Dubois Riverside Cott 3 Silverton Lane ROTHBURY NE65 9NB
Our ref Cat04/JT/D450 Please use the heading FITNESS FOR ALL

Your ref   ED/MF

Mark this PERSONAL

Dr Mrs Dubois

We are pleased to enclose our new fitness cat, which you requested last month. We apologise for the delay, due to printing problems, but are sure you will appreshiate the quality of our firms' products and feel the inconveniance was worthwhile.

Our equipment *,of the highest quality and value,* is suitable for any level of fitness. A ~~trim~~ and healthy body is an acheivable way to improve your self-esteem. Investing in the correct exercise equipment to use in your own home is an efficient way of utilising your time and avoiding expencive club fees.

Each item of equipment comes with full details for assembly, *a recomended exercise programme* and *instructions for use*. All parts are covered by our comprehensive co gntee.

A seperate order form is enclosed for ~~mail order your use~~. To find a product type, simply key the item code into the search box at the top of the page and click on 'go'. You will receive an e-mail acknowledging receipt of your order and giving you despatch info.

In the unlikely event that you need to return any goods, details of how to do this are given on the despatch note. We are confident that you will find the equipment to suit your requirements and look forward to being of service to you.

Alternatively you may use our secure online service at www.fitfun.com.

Yrs sncly

Jo Tuck
Marketing

21

Exercise 2.3

Key in this exercise using a letterheading from the CD. Amend as shown and correct all word errors and 2 errors of agreement. Print a copy and check it with the worked example on page 114.

Letter to Mr and Mrs Johnston 12 Market Sq FOLKESTONE Kent CT20 4PO
Our ref PdeH/C5811 Please use the heading TEMPTING TRIPS

Your ref 72811

(Mark this PRIORITY)

Dear Mr and Mrs Johnston

As it is ~~some time quite long~~ since yr last holiday with us, you might ✓ like some info on the new holidays our org have just introduced.

The forign travel/includes ,which may appeal to you, destinations such as a tour thrugh Borneos' rainforests and a journey across Bulgaria.

We also offer new luxury cruises to Greenland and South America on board ships exclusively used by our co.

(Inset this paragraph 50mm from left margin)
New special interest holidays feature in the enclosed cat, such as photography in Vietnam and modern jazz in Portugal.

(emphasise this paragraph)
Flights to most destinations can be ~~booked through~~ arranged from a choice of ✓ 15 regional airports. Accommodation is provided for single travellers at no extra cost. These includes insurance and travel accessories.

We also enclose a leaflet advertiseing misc products and services available from our order dept. By completing and returning the questionnaire on the back page, you can ensure that you will recieve details from us of only those items that are of interest to you. It will gntee you entry into our prize draw, where you will have a chance to win £1,000 worth of vouchers' to spend on your next holiday with us or on goods from the leaflet, if you prefer.

We look forward to hearing from you soon, as we are confident that you will find a holiday to tempt you.

Yours sncly

Peta De Haan
Manager

Memos

Layout and style

You will need to produce a memo in the text production exam. Any style of heading may be used. You may key in your own heading or recall a template provided on the CD-ROM.

You may need to remind yourself of the layout and requirements for a memo in the exams, as at this level *the memo details are not set out for you.*

The following example is in fully blocked style (each line starts at the left margin), with open punctuation. This is the style used in OCR text processing exams. At least one clear linespace should be left between each separate item, with equal spacing between paragraphs.

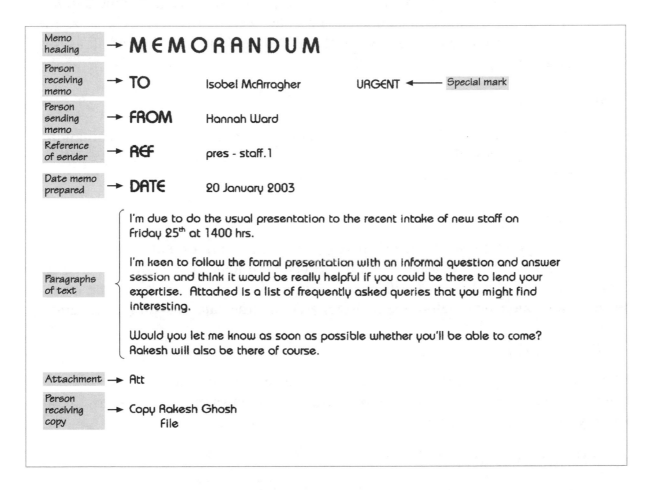

Entries against side headings

If you chose to design a template for recall you may wish to insert infill points alongside the headings.

TO   * (infill point)
FROM   * (infill point)

In the exam, if you use such a design, you must remember to delete these symbols when keying in the details, otherwise you will lose marks. The TO and FROM headings are sometimes transposed in the exam document. It is important to check that you are entering the correct details against the headings.

The following styles are also acceptable in the exam.

Leaving equal spaces	Leaving unequal spaces	Using tab stop	
TO Peter Parkes	TO Peter Parkes	TO	Peter Parkes
FROM Fay Hawkes	FROM Fay Hawkes	FROM	Fay Hawkes

Remember to use the mouse or cursor keys to move between the headings to avoid creating extra linespaces.

Reference

This should be copied *exactly* as it is on the draft, following spacing, punctuation and capitalisation. It should be aligned against the heading in the same way as the other details. If no reference is shown in the draft one should not be added, as this will incur a penalty.

Date

The same rules apply as given for business letters and each memo must contain a date. No instruction will be given on the draft but, in the exam, a reminder will be given on the front cover of the question paper.

Special mark

In the exam, you will be instructed to key in a special mark on either the memo or letter. The special mark is used to signify special treatment of the document, eg *By Hand, Personal, Private and Confidential, Urgent*. For exam purposes, in the memo it is acceptable anywhere before the main text. Follow the capitalisation in the draft.

Enclosure(s)

The same rules apply as those given for business letters, although strictly speaking the use of *Att* (for attachment) is normally more correct than *Enc* as memos are not usually delivered in envelopes.

Continuation sheet

The same rules apply as those given for business letters.

Correction of errors/correction signs/abbreviations

Full details are given in the information about business letters. The same rules apply to the memo. **Remember that errors of agreement are only tested in document 2, which is usually the memo.**

Postdating

The same rules apply as those given for business letters.

Incorporating information

You may come across the following tests in either document 2 or 3.

You will need to find a one-word item from a previous document in order to complete the missing word. For example, *Mrs W_____* in the memo draft may be found to be a *Mrs Wentworth* when you check with the letter and so you simply key in the complete word.

There will be an instruction to find an item from another document and incorporate it into the document you are working on. For example, the draft may look like this:

The shop is open from please add opening times here every day except Sunday.

When you check with another document, you find that the times are 0900 hrs to 1730 hrs and so you simply key the information in the correct position. It will then read:

The shop is open from 0900 hrs to 1730 hrs every day except Sunday.

It is important to make sure that you include *all* the necessary words.

The following exercises will give you extra practice in the above features before you attempt a full practice exam. When using the memo heading from the CD, you may find that the text you key against the side headings follows the style of those headings. Although this is accepted in the exam, you may want to format this text so that it matches the paragraphs of text in the rest of the document.

Exercise 2.4

Key in this exercise using a memo heading from the CD. Amend as shown and correct all word errors and 3 errors of agreement. The item of information you need to add can be found in Exercise 2.1 (in this section). Print a copy and check it with the worked example on page 116.

Memo from Iain Duncan to Judy Blum
Ref ID/IB62

I have just drafted the attached letter to a Mrs M——.
I should like a similar letters sent out to each cleint on our database who do not currently hold an Internet a/c.

You will need to ensure that we have suficient leaflets to send out with this mail shot.

① I am ~~starting a~~ ~~planning the~~ staff training session on our new spreadsheet software on Wed (give date for first Wed of next month). Initially I am asking section heads to recomend a member of their team to attend this first session, which will run from 1000 hrs to 1200 hrs. //Further training will be arranged as necy and I am asking all interested staff to contact you. ↓ I am sure that staff trained in the first session will share their knowledge with coleagues in their sections, althogh I beleive many person will [people] prefer to be given the opp to take part in a formal training session.

Please start a list so that we can find out the demand.

Exercise 2.5

Key in this exercise using a memo heading from the CD. Amend as shown and correct all word errors and errors of agreement. You can find the items of information you need to add in the business letter Exercise 2.2 (in this section). Print a copy and check it with the worked example on page 117.

> Memo from Jo Tuck to Nan Moretti
> Ref JT/MP.launch

> Insert the same heading as used in the letter to Mrs Dubois

I am pleased /to confirm/ that the printing problems have been resolved and we are now able to send the new cat out. The address for ordering online is w——.

We are about to launch a sophisticated range of equipment, which have an amazing number of electronic features. // Attached /for your info/ is a copy of the advertisment that will appeared in the usual magazines and periodicals.

The official launch evening has been ~~booked at~~ arranged with Park Hotel ✓ for Fri (give date for last Fri of next month). I will ask yr sec to make an appt for (you) to give (me) the usual briefing prior to the event.

I am out of the office tomorrow, attending the comittee monitoring the safety aspects of fitness equipment.

One of the items on the agenda are the effect of the new European Union legislation. Rest assured that I shall report back to you immed with any findings or recomendations that may affect our busness.

Exercise 2.6

Key in this exercise using a memo heading from the CD. Amend as shown and correct all word errors and errors of agreement. You can find the items of information you need to add in the business letter Exercise 2.3 (in this section). Print a copy and check it with the worked example on page 118.

Memo from Peta De Haan to Jamie Cullum
Ref PdeH/Sm

I attach a copy for your info.

Mark this URGENT

I think the current ~~brochure~~ *leaflet* advertiseing our travel products ✓ and services need redrafting. The format looks rather uninteresting and would benefit from *the addition of* some colourful graphics.

I should prefer the draft on the prize draw, where cleints have the chance to win £ ___, to be moved to the middle of the leaflet. This would improve the impact and it could be printed on a 'tear-out' pages. *from it's current back page position*

~~I am keen to promote the special interest holidays in our new cat.~~ Could you work on a flyer that can be inserted in the updated leaflet? I should like the new special interest holidays' featured in our cat, such as (please add details here), to be given star billing.

I should apreciate an opp to meet up next week ~~we shall need to get together as soon as poss~~ to go thru the advertiseing material needed for the trade fair in Birmingham in 2 month's time. I know that a great deal of work on these have already been completed by your team! Please ring Sally to fix a suitable date when we are both available.

and I am looking forward to seeing the new material

Articles and reports

Layout and style

You will need to produce an article or report for the text production exam. Plain A4 paper should be used and the font should be easily read. Times New Roman or Arial in 10 to 12 pitch are popular with examiners. The paragraphs in the exam drafts are always in blocked style. Continuation sheets should be numbered.

Linespacing

Follow the linespacing indicated in the draft document regarding spacing after headings and between paragraphs. Make sure that you are consistent throughout the document. Remind yourself of the basic rules given in Section 1.

Instructions are given in the exam to change linespacing from single to double, or vice versa, for a small section of text or for the majority of a document. You may prefer to leave such alterations until you have finished keying in the document.

Insetting

You may be instructed to inset a portion of text from the left margin. The measurements must be exact or else you will lose marks. The safest way to ensure an exact measurement is to use **Format→Paragraph→Indents and Spacing→Indentation Left** or **Right** select the measurement you need→**OK**.

Word errors, spellings and abbreviations

Remember that, at this level, words that contain typographical (keying in) or spelling errors, as well as abbreviations that require expanding, will not be circled.

Correction signs

You must amend the text you key in according to the correction signs given in Section 1.

Emphasising text

Instructions are often given in this document to emphasise a heading, sentence or paragraph. Any of the following methods or any combination of them is acceptable:

- capitalisation
- underlining
- change of font to bold or italic
- change of font style and/or size
- change of linespacing
- centring
- insetting from left margin.

Headings

Follow draft regarding capitalisation and spacing of headings. Their style and the linespacing before and after should be consistent throughout the document. Headings should have at least one clear linespace before and after them but should not be on a different page from the start of their related paragraphs. You may have to insert a hard page break to ensure this (instructions given in Section 1).

Footnotes

In this exam you are required to insert two footnotes in the report or article. **Each footnote must appear on the same page as the symbol in the relevant text.** There should be no space between the word and symbol in the text, but one space should be left between the symbol[1] and the footnote, as shown on this page.

The footnote text is designed to remain at the foot of the relevant page and not be incorporated into the paragraph text. It is important that footnotes are not omitted, as this would incur heavy penalties.

How to add a footnote

Make sure you are working in **Page Layout View**. Position your cursor immediately after the word in the text that requires a footnote. From the menu bar use **Insert→Footnote**. The following dialogue box appears:

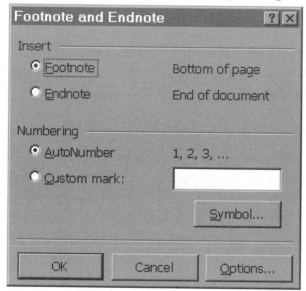

Figure 2.1 Footnote and Endnote dialogue box

Take care to select **Footnote** and not Endnote. **AutoNumber** will automatically be selected. Click **OK**. This will place a small number after the word in the text and at the bottom of the page (ready for the footnote to be keyed in). Any number or symbol is acceptable in the exam.

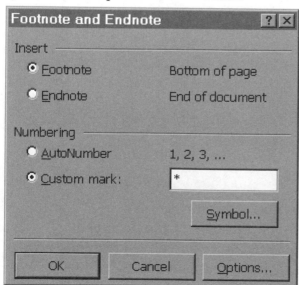

Figure 2.2 Selecting footnote number or symbol

[1] This may be customised as * , ** or ᵃ , ᵇ or any other relevant symbol

If you prefer to use a symbol, such as the asterisk shown here in the dialogue box, click on **Symbol**, select the **Font**, click the symbol you require, then **OK**. If you have two footnotes in your document, you will need to select the asterisk twice at this stage.

A footnote pane will open at the end of your page (as on page 30) for you to key in your footnote text.

When you have finished keying your footnote text, just move your cursor back to your main text and continue with your document. You can add more than one footnote to the same page by simply repeating the steps given above.

Distraction element

In the exam, 15–20 minutes after the start the invigilator will announce two items of information for you to add to the report or article.

For example, the invigilator will say: *Here is the information for document 3 – The contestants received bottles of wine and lottery tickets. A sum of £7,000 has been added to the budget figures.* Write down this dictated material immediately on the inside of your exam answer folder, so that it is available for easy reference when you need it. In document 3 the places where you need to add the missing information to the text are shown by dashes, eg *Contestants received bottles of wine* ___ ___ ___ and *The club has added a sum of* ___ *to the budget figures.* Once you have keyed in the missing words, the text will read *Contestants received bottles of wine and lottery tickets* and *The club has added a sum of £7,000 to the budget figures.*

The following exercises will give you extra practice in the above features before you attempt a full practice exam. The items of information for dictation are given at the top of each exercise. If possible, ask someone to dictate them to you 5 minutes after you start the exercise. Otherwise, simply copy them from your book.

Exercise 2.7

Key in this exercise, amending as shown and correcting all word errors. Print a copy and check it with the worked example on pages 119–20. The two dictated items of information you need for this document are: The festival pays a subscription to the Performing Rights Society. A solo performance no longer than 10 minutes does not need permission.

ARTS FESTIVAL CONDITIONS

Double linespacing except where indicated

Eligibility

The competitions are intended for amateurs, but professionals ma6y take part as conductors or accompanists.

Adjudicators may not judge a claass in which any of their pupils are competing.

SCheduling

emphasise this sentence only

Entrants wil be given at least 2 week's notice of the dates and times of competition classes. Entry fees will only be returned if a class is with drawn.

No entries will be accepted after Mon *(give date for last Mon of next month)* and no alterations to competitors chosen pieces will be accepted after this date.

Judging and Marking

A high standard is expected from performers and our judges will mark accordingly. Their decision is final. // Any complaints should be made in writing to the festival sec immed after the performance.

of charge

Mark sheets an certificates may be obtained free at the end of each class. They are awarded in accordance with national standards[1] as follows:

1   Performance - 75%[2] (aged under 12)

2   Merit - 81%

3 4 Distinction - 87%

4 3 Commended - 84%

5   Honours - 90%

All awards will be presented at the final concert.

[1] British and International Federation of Festivals

[2] Aged 12 and over - 78%

<u>Copyright</u>

These paragraphs only in single linespacing

with the appropriate body

An agreement has been reached / that permission is not necy for the solo performance of poetry or prose lasting no longer than — minutes.

Gruop drama is not covered by this ~~agreement~~ and it is up to the performers to obtain the relevant permits befroe submitting entries.

Amateur scripts or pieces of music are nott affected, so no official permission needs to be sought other than an acknowledgement to the author or composer.

<u>Permissions</u>

The festival pays a subscription to the ___ ___ ___ and advises them of every piece of music to be performed. Individual competitors do not need to obtain copyright for any of their chosen music.

Exercise 2.8

Key in this exercise, amending as shown and correcting all word errors. Print a copy and check it with the worked example on pages 121–23. The two dictated items of information you need for this document are: In summer a wet or dry suit should be 3 mm thick. Avoid sailing 3 or 4 hours after high or low tide.

WATERSPORT SAFETY ← *Centre this heading*

Double linespacing except where indicated

Windsurfing can be safely enjoyed by almost anyone, by following a few basic guidelines.

Inset this section of text 50 mm from left margin

1   Learn to windsurf at a recognised centre

2   Wear suitable clothing and beware off the cold

3   Always wear a buoyancy aid and harness

4   Maintain you equipment

~~8~~ 7   Never sail alone

~~6~~ 5   Follow local advice regarding tides and winds

~~7~~ 6   Practice emergency procedures

<u>Correct Training</u>

and techniques involved,

As well as learning the skill/you need to be taught basic principles about ~~self preservation~~ *self-rescue* ✓ and precautions to take with equipment. *A recognised centre that is registered with the Royal Yachting Association will ensure you are properly trained.*

leading to hypothermia, weakness and delayed reactions

<u>Personal Aids</u>

Activity in water causes rapid loss of body heat. In summer a wet or dry suit ——— thick is the minimum requirement. In winter it should have a thickness of 5 mm or more. Be aware of posible heat loss, especially if the winds are blowing from the north or east. Most heat is lost from the head, hands and feet and <u>in cold weather</u> therefore a hat,[1] gloves and boots are advisable. Woolly hats are not recommended.

<u>Clothing</u>

Although a wet suit will provide some buoyancy, it is advisable to wear a specially designed aid and harness which do not impede your movements. *As you progress to wave jumping or speed sailing, a crash helmet will be required.*

[1] *A tight-fitting neoprene hat is the best.*

Equipment

It is vital to ensure that all parts of your board and rig are in good order. Pay particular attention to ropes, pulleys, universal joints and connections, mast, boom, and safety leashes. Rinse metal parts in fresh water at teh end of each session.

These paragraphs only in single linespacing

Weather

Listen to the weather forecast and take advice from the local coastguards, windsurfing shops or sailors about currents and suitable beaches. Never windsurf in fog or at night.

A wind blowing away from the shore is deceptive and dangerous. Choose a beach where the wind blows parallel to the coast, or slightly towards the shore. Never sail in an offshore wind. *(emphasise this sentence only)*

The safest time is at the turn of the tide. Avoid sailing — — — — after high or low tide, when the speed of the water flow is at it's fastest.

Another recognised signal is slowly raised and lowered outstretched arms.

Emergency Procedures

Be prepared fro the worst and always carry an orange smoke signal or red distress flare strapped to your wetsuit. Attract attention immediately. Never leave your board, as it will help to keep you afloat. If you are experienced and confident, attempt self-rescue.[2] Alternatively, keeep warm and paddle to maintain your position. ONce you are safely back on the beach, inform the coastguard.

Use the 'Buddy' System

Do not be tempted to sail alone - always go out with a 'buddy'. Make sure that your exp[ected time of return is known by someone ashore and that they keep visual contact with you on the water. If possible, choose a beach with rescue cover. ~~Belonging to a~~ *Clubs will provide a friendly means of practising your sport.* ~~club will give you plenty of people to go out with.~~

[2] *Techniques taught by the RYA.*

Exercise 2.9

Key in this exercise, amending as shown and correcting all word errors. Print a copy and check it with the worked example on pages 124–26. The two dictated items of information you need for this document are: The firm has been established for 15 years. The firm is a member of The Guild of Master Craftsmen.

THE POND PEOPLE ← (Centre this heading)

What We Offer

We specialise in creating features that are designed to enhance your garden as well as attract wildlife. We are an expanding firm of dedicated ecologists offering the following services.

1   Pond design and construction with adjacent/ *hard and soft* landscaping

2   Pump and filter installation, wit associated electrical work

3   Hard landscaping - paving, patios and paths

4   Consultancy wok on existing ponds and environments

~~5~~ 6   Wildlife garden design, construction and planting

~~6~~ 7   Maintenance service on all the above

~~7~~ 5   Cleaning repairs and re-stocking

More About Us

Our co biologists conduct original research into freshwater environments and ecological systems. Our installation teams are staffed by experienced builders and electricians.*

We have been established for — years and have worked for the private, commercial and public sectors on large and small projects. We act as consultants for organisations and arrange lectures. We work with conservation groups, schools, businesses and clubs.

They are recognised experts in their particular fields.

Water Works

THe key to a successful pond is careful p;lanting. We will suggest a plant list of specific types and numbers to suit your particular water feature and attract wildlife.

We will advise you of the optimum shape and depth for the size you require, and where to site it.

* Members of Federation of Master Builders

On a summers' day a well-balanced pond ~~can be~~ is a fascinating sight: dragonflies darting around the margins, pondskaters skimming the surface, frogs leaping in and uot of the water. Birds will enjoy drinking and bathing in the shallows. ✓

These paragraphs only in single linespacing

<u>Why Choose Us?</u>

Wildlife gardening is based on the concept that the most likely way of attracting birds, insects and animals into your graden is by using native plants.

In our planting wee take in to a/c the conditions ~~existing~~ ~~prevailing~~ in a particular area and use plants that would occur in similar places in the wild. ✓

A bird shrubbery and mixed hedgerows are habitats that can be created in all but the smallest gardens.

<u>Wild Ways</u>

, butterfly border, wild flower meadow

We are dedicated to nature conservation and caring for the environment. We offer a rare combination of practical expertise and scientific knowledge.**

(Emphasise this paragraph)

As a member of — — — — —, our firm takes great pride in its work and can gntee that you will be pleased and satisfied with the results.

Contact us on 01737 346394 and let us improve your environment.

** Six staff members hold science degrees

Section 3

Word processing

This exam must be word processed and completed within $1^3/_4$ hours. You have to produce four documents: a report/article, a table, a newspaper column article and a letter or memo.

Your work must contain no more than 14 faults overall to achieve a pass and no more than 5 faults overall to gain a distinction. Practice exams are provided in Section 4.

In this section you will practise the following skills which are tested in the exam:

- Adjusting line length and justifying text
- Altering linespacing
- Changing font type and size
- Insetting text from both margins and leaving vertical and horizontal space
- Emphasising, underlining, centring text
- Sorting lists into alphabetical, numerical and chronological order
- Interpreting amendment and correction signs (given in Section 1)
- Selecting and incorporating information from another document and a resource sheet
- Selecting and inserting paragraphs into a document from another file
- Changing specified words automatically by using search and replace facility
- Checking and amending an incorrect item of information
- Moving and copying text by using cut/copy and paste facility
- Inserting headers and footers and automatic page numbering
- Altering existing page breaks and inserting new ones
- Presenting information in newspaper columns
- Presenting information in a ruled landscaped table with a variable number of columns
- Producing extra copies and showing routing

You will already have acquired many of the skills you need and some, such as layout of business letters and memos, are similar to those required for the text production exam and are covered in detail in Section 2.

Recall text for the practice exercises in this section is available on the CD-ROM.

Articles and reports

Layout and style

You will need to produce an article or report for the word processing exam. Recall text for this document will be in Times New Roman 12 pitch or Arial 11 pitch with a ragged left margin and blocked paragraphs. You will be instructed to alter the line length and linespacing and to use a justified right margin, skills which you will have already practised. Plain A4 paper should be used for your printout and continuation sheets should be numbered.

Linespacing

Instructions are given to change the linespacing from single to double, or vice versa, for the majority of this document. There is also an instruction to alter the linespacing for one portion of text. You may prefer to leave such alterations until you have finished amending the text.

Insetting

In this document you will be instructed to inset a section of text an exact amount from both left and right margins. The measurements must be exact or else a penalty will be incurred. The safest way to ensure an exact measurement is to mark the text, then click **Format→Paragraph →Indents and Spacing →Indentation Left** and **Right** key the measurements you need→**OK**. Be careful that you inset only the section indicated.

Page breaks

The recall text for this document contains two hard page breaks. You are instructed to delete these and insert three page breaks in different places. This is simply done by deleting each existing **Page Break** instruction that is revealed when the ¶ **(Show/Hide)** icon is clicked, moving your cursor to the position for each new page break, holding down **Control** and pressing **Enter**. Section 1 gives detailed information about page breaks.

Correction signs

You must amend the text in accordance with the correction signs given in Section 1.

Headings

Follow the rules that are given in Section 2.

Headers and footers

You will already be familiar with this facility, but at this level you are instructed to insert both a header and a footer on every page of this document.

Use **View→Header and Footer**. The header box will appear at the top of the page.

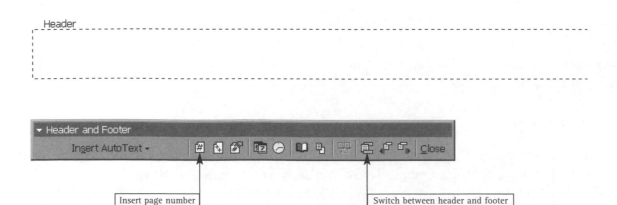

Figure 3.1 Adding header

Key in the given header text in the left side of the box. It is a good idea to add your name or candidate details on the right side of the box.

Next, click the **Switch Between Header and Footer** icon, which will make the footer box appear at the bottom of the page. Key in the given footer text in the left side of the box. To add page numbers, move the cursor to the right of the box and click on the **Automatic Page Numbering** icon, then click **Close**.

Search and replace

You are asked to find instances of a repeated word and change them to another throughout the document. You will already know how to use the automatic facility of **Edit→Replace** to carry this out efficiently.

Moving and copying text

You will be instructed to move and copy different sections of text to another page within the document.

Use the **Cut** and **Paste** icons to MOVE a section of text, so that it appears *once* in the document.

Use the **Copy** and **Paste** icons to COPY a section of text, so that it appears *twice* in the document.

Sort

You may be instructed to sort a list into alphabetical, numerical or chronological (date) order in this document. You will already know how to use **Table→Sort** select **Ascending,** to carry this out quickly and easily. Check that the listed items are aligned and have the same linespacing between them.

The following exercises will give you extra practice in the above features before you attempt a full practice exam.

Exercise 3.1

Recall this exercise from the CD–ROM and amend as shown. Adjust the margins to give a line length of 13 cm. Change to double linespacing (except where indicated) and use full justification. Insert and delete page breaks so that the document prints on 3 pages. Insert MONEY BAGS PLC as a header and Forward Planning as a footer, to appear on every page. Print a copy and check it with the worked example on pages 127–28.

Our company offers its services specifically to people over the age of 50.

Economic Climate

We aim to help our customers arrange their finances in order to reduce reliance upon any one factor, thus reducing risks and improving yields.

and low interest rates on savings

The current situation, with unpredictable stock markets, makes investing difficult.

Consultants

All of our advisers have experience with reputable financial institutions. They receive regular training and assessment to ensure they maintain our high standards.

assessed on

Our consultants are ~~rewarded for~~ the quality of their recommendations and the standard ✓ of service they provide, based on feedback from customers they have advised.

Page 2 starts here

Advice

B

covering such matters as

We offer a wide range of services to customers, ~~including the following topics~~

bonds
annuities
assurances
inheritance tax
income protection
investment trusts
pension planning
savings accounts
unit trusts

This section only in single linespacing

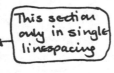

Sort into exact alphabetical order

Page 3 starts here

If you have existing investments to invest or a lump sum you wish to review, we can help you to achieve income or growth, or a combination of both. If you are due to retire in the near future, we can show you how to maximise your income through careful investing.

Inset this section of text 25mm from both left and right margins

You may decide to make provision for the costs of long term care. We can help you to plan for the potential burden of residential or nursing care.

Copy to (A)

Money Bags plc is an Independent Financial Adviser, committed to offering straightforward, unbiased advice.

Move to (B)

If you need financial advice, one of our consultants can help you to decide on a course of action, taking into account your complete circumstances, requirements and objectives.

Change customers to clients throughout this document

Exercise 3.2

Recall this exercise from the CD-ROM and amend as shown. Adjust the margins to give a line length of 11 cm. Change to double linespacing (except where indicated) and use full justification. Insert and delete page breaks so that the document prints on 3 pages. Insert CAREER MANAGEMENT as a header and Young People as a footer, to appear on every page. Print a copy and check it with the worked example on pages 130–32.

Copy to △

Our main purpose is to give independent guidance and information on careers. We also provide a job placing service for younger people leaving education and for those already in the labour market.

Guidance

We help our clients to identify their aims, understand the opportunities open to them and recognise the possibilities of lifelong learning and training.

Many of our objectives are achieved through liaising with other organisations such as

Employment groups
Employers' organisations
Learning and skills councils
District councils
Support agencies
Schools and colleges
Voluntary organisations

Sort into exact alphabetical order

Page 2 starts here

This section only in single linespacing

Labour Market

Advisers work in schools and colleges to offer individual interviews, group work and drop-in sessions.//Consultants will attend parent and open evenings and provide leaflets and software for students and parents. ▼Advice is offered to those who may need to adjust their plans in the light of exam results.

Education

Training and support is also offered to teachers and tutors.

Those already in employment can drop into one of the offices or, if they prefer, phone or e-mail for an appointment.

We have lending libraries of software packages on personal development and career information in all of our local offices.

Move to ▢

We give advice on career routes, current job and training vacancies and information about trends in the market that are likely to affect employment.

Support

Help with CVs, letters of application and interview technique is given.

Aptitude and skill testing is offered to help people ~~realise~~ *identify* their personal strengths and weaknesses. ✓

(Page 3 starts here)

Employers

opportunities in training and

We advise employers about the labour market situation locally. Our expertise is available to help match young people to vacancies.

The assistance we give employers includes displaying job advertisements in our offices and sending flyers out to interested parties.

Inset this section of text 15mm from left and right margins

Other Services

Working within the spheres of Education and employment, we are uniquely qualified to offer an insight into what happens to people when they leave full time education.

We are well informed about trends in the market and about new government initiatives, ~~together~~ with changes in qualifications and training routes. We are therefore able to offer statistics and guidance on all such matters.

Change offices to centres throughout this document

44

Exercise 3.3

Recall this exercise from the CD-ROM and amend as shown. Adjust the margins to give a line length of 12 cm. Change to double linespacing (except where indicated) and use full justification. Insert and delete page breaks so that the document prints on 4 pages. Print a copy and check it with the worked example on pages 133–36.

NOT IN MY BACKYARD!

Emissions *Copy to ⊛*

This agency has been set up to provide easy access for the public to information about industrial pollution locally and nationally.

It helps to regulate industry and aids the government in its obligations and commitments.

Our Mission

details of

Our pollution inventory contains ~~information on~~ chemical and radioactive emissions from industrial locations *nationwide in the* ~~following~~ *sectors:* ✓

Fuel and power production
Material manufacture
Manufactured white goods
Chemical production
Mineral processes
Metal production
Sewage treatment
Waste disposal

Page 2 starts here

Sort into exact alphabetical order

This section only in single linespacing

Data from landfill locations, waste transfer stations and treatment plants was added to the inventory in *January 2003*.

Other sectors, such as intensive agriculture and food and drink, must report to the agency within the next 5 years.

Smaller scale activities, such as incineration and spraying, are regulated by local authorities.

Move to ⓞ

To access the inventory, click on www.pollagent.gov.uk. Information for a particular area can be found through data maps or by keying in a postcode, place name or grid reference.

Change locations to sites throughout this document

Collecting Data

The operators of industrial locations are responsible for reporting emissions of each substance per year.

This must include both planned and accidental releases, although ~~operators are required to report just~~ those that exceed a set threshold level. *data is only needed for*

Page 3 starts here

Accessing Data

⊚ *Inset this section of text 40mm from both left and right margins*

You can also search using criteria such as name of operator, year of interest, type of process and substances released.

, including a breakdown of figures,
Statistics are available from 1999 onwards showing discharges from outlets such as chimneys, vents, discharge pipes, leaks and spillages.

Page 4 starts here

Future

✱

Our role will expand over the next few years. European legislation requires us to implement new regulations to cover a wide range of activities including landfills, intensive agriculture and the ~~food~~ and drink industries.

What is in our backyard concerns us all!

Insert WASTE WATCH as a header and People Power as a ~~footer~~. Header and ~~footer~~ to appear on every page

Articles in newspaper style

Layout and style

You will need to produce a two column newspaper style article on plain A4 paper for the word processing exam. In the following practice exercises, the recall text for this document is drafted using the default line length. You will need to format the edited text into two columns.

Formatting columns

Complete any additional keying in and editing of the text before formatting it into columns. This makes the document easier to handle and check against the original draft. It is easier to work with columns in **Print Layout View**, otherwise the columns are displayed underneath each other on the screen rather than side by side.

To format the columns use **Format→Columns** select 2 and **Whole Document→OK**. The dialogue box should look like this:

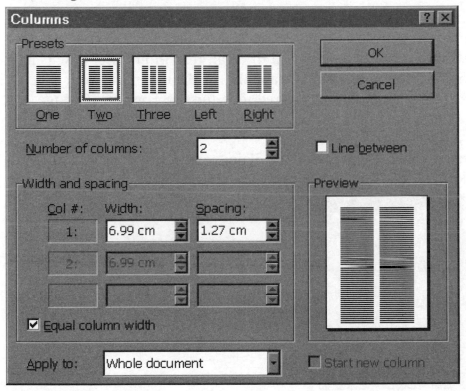

Figure 3.2 Columns dialogue box

You do not have to make the column lengths equal, but you may add extra linespacing to make the second column start on the same line as the first, if you wish.

Linespacing

Follow copy regarding linespacing before and after headings and between paragraphs. Consistency within each document is important.

Vertical and horizontal spacing

In the following exercises and in one of the exam documents you are instructed to *leave a vertical space at least . . . mm across from left margin by . . . mm but no more than . . . mm across by . . . mm down.* This sounds very complicated, but is quite easy to format using the ruler lines and/or **Format→Indents and Spacing**. It is simpler to insert such spacing once the text has been formatted into columns. The spacing does not have to be exact, but must fall within the given measurements. The horizontal space should be measured from the left margin. The vertical space may be measured from text to text or may include the space above and/or below the paragraph alongside the instruction. **The resulting box-shaped space should not be ruled.**

Font style and size

In this document an instruction may be given to *change the typeface and/or pitch size* of a section of recall text. Use **Format→Font** and select **Font** and **Size**, making sure that your choice can be easily read.

Capitalisation

You may also be instructed to change a section of recall text from lower case (small letters with initial capitals) to upper case (all capitals), or the other way round. A simple way to format this is to mark the required text and use **Format→Change Case.**

If you are altering lower case to upper case, the dialogue box will appear as follows and you simply click **OK:**

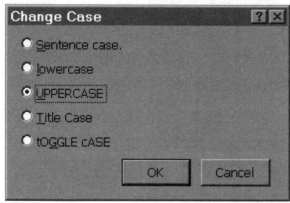

Figure 3.3 Changing text to upper case

If you are altering upper case to lower case, make sure you select **Sentence case** (small letters with initial capitals at the start of each sentence). The dialogue box should look like this:

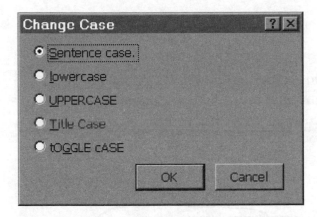

Figure 3.4 Changing text to lower case

It is important to remember that initial capitals for proper nouns (names of people or places) will not be retained, so you will need to alter any of these individually.

Incorporating information

In one document in the word processing exam you will be instructed to copy *part* of a previously stored document into your file. It is important that you copy only the section asked for, as you will lose marks for any redundant text.

To copy part of a stored document to the one you are working on, carry out the following steps:

- **Save** the document you are working on (less risk of losing work if you make an error).
- Keeping your current document open, click the **Open** icon and select the name of the file from which you want to copy the text, click the **Open** tab on the bottom right of the box (the 2nd file appears on your screen while your original document remains open beneath it).
- **Mark** carefully just the section of text to be copied, click the **Copy** icon and then close this file (your original document will remain on the screen).
- Place your cursor at the point where you want to insert the copied text, click the **Paste** icon.
- The copied text should now be in the correct place. If necessary alter your linespacing or font to make sure that it is consistent with the rest of your document.

The following exercises will give you extra practice in the above features before you attempt a full practice exam.

Exercise 3.4

Recall this exercise from the CD-ROM and amend as shown, retaining the abbreviations. Display the whole document in 2 columns (newspaper style). Print a copy and check it with the worked example on page 137.

PASSPORT PROTOCOL

Your passport is an important means of identification. Make sure that it is kept in a secure place at all times. When travelling abroad, place it in a hotel safe whenever possible.

To travel abroad you should hold a passport that is valid for at least 6 months. Make sure you apply in plenty of time. You may also need a visa to enter certain countries outside the European Union.

Change this paragraph to upper case

You must report the loss or theft of your passport without delay to the police and the UKPS, or, if you are abroad, to the British consulate, embassy or high commission.

To reduce the possibility of misuse, you will be required to complete and sign a declaration form. This is available from your local police station or post office, or by ringing the advice line on 0870 521 0410.

computer data relating to your

Upon receiving formal notification of loss, the document is flagged as cancelled. It cannot be reinstated even if your passport subsequently turns up. *In this case you should return the document to the UKPS, to ensure its permanent removal from circulation.*

Change the typeface and/or pitch size for this paragraph only

To avoid delaying your future travel plans, you should apply for a replacement document as soon as you discover your loss.

Make a note of your passport number and date of issue and ensure you complete the next of kin details inside. *Before going abroad, leave a copy of these details with a friend or relative at home and take a second means of photographic identification with you.*

Both your identity and the document are open to misuse should it be lost or stolen.

Exercise 3.5

Recall this exercise from the CD-ROM and amend as shown. Display the whole document in 2 columns (newspaper style). Remember to carry out the spacing instruction once you have formatted the columns. Print a copy and check it with the worked example on page 138.

SAILING BARGE CHARTER

Change this sentence to lower case

CHARTER ONE OF OUR THAMES SAILING BARGES FOR A DAY OUT WITH A DIFFERENCE.

Leave a space here at least 35 mm across from left margin and 35 mm down but no more than 45 mm across and 45mm down. DO NOT RULE BOX.

You can take a trip up the River Swale and enjoy watching the seals sun themselves on the estuary sandbanks.

Alternatively, you may prefer to cruise around the North Kent coast, *spotting familiar landmarks and* visiting the forts that were built as sea defences during the second world war.

We can organise lunch for you, if you wish. This would consist of a picnic hamper made up especially for your party and supplied by a local caterer.

You are welcome to bring your own food and drink. Galley facilities are available, but most of our passengers prefer to bring a picnic so that they can concentrate on the sailing rather than the cooking!

Our barges carry a crew of 4: the skipper, mate and 2 seamen. *We only take small groups and require 10-15 people for a day's charter.*

Before departure we serve hot soup, *and rolls, coffee and cakes* and brief you about the barge and its safety regulations.

Change the typeface and/or pitch size for this paragraph only

We use our engine to move from our mooring, but once underway, the sails are set, the engine cut and peace and calm descends.

We can anchor at interesting locations for lunch, or you can eat underway. If you fancy trying your hand at winding the anchor or hauling in the sails or leeboards, the skipper will welcome your help.

However, there is no obligation to participate and you may prefer to sit back, drink and doze and let the scenery slip by you.

Why not give us a ring on 01795 678419 for further details? We shall be delighted to show you around a barge and below decks before you make a booking.

Refrigeration is installed, so you can cool your beer or wine.

Exercise 3.6

Recall this exercise from the CD-ROM and amend as shown. You are required to copy part of a pre-stored document and insert it into this exercise. Check the instructions carefully to make sure you do this correctly. Display the whole document in 2 columns (newspaper style). Print a copy and check it with the worked example on page 139.

EN-ABLE

Leave a space here at least 45mm across from left margin and 50mm down but no more than 50mm across and 60mm down. DO NOT RULE BOX.

En-Able offers a range of computer-based courses that will help you to improve your career prospects.

Whether you want to brush up your skills before returning to work, prepare for promotion or for a move to a new job, we have the package for you.

Our database covers most areas of employment and recognised qualifications. You can choose your style from full or part time and self or tutor aided study.

just a few options from

The following list shows/the wide range of modular courses we offer.

Business studies
Counselling
Childcare
Computing
Complementary therapies
English
Mathematics
Languages
Sport and leisure
Teaching

Please sort this list into exact alphabetical order

Change this section to lower case

Copy the 3rd paragraph from the document stored as COURSES and insert here

WE HAVE MORE THAN 1,500 CENTRES THROUGHOUT GREAT BRITAIN. THEY ARE LOCATED IN LIBRARIES, COMMUNITY AND SPORTS CENTRES AND IN THE HIGH STREETS OF MAJOR TOWNS.

You can even work from home, as long as you have access to the Internet.

We will discuss the various options with you and help you to choose the path that is best suited to your requirements.

For free advice, call us on 0800 198 276 from 0800 hrs - 2200 hrs, 7 days a week.

Our courses are uniquely flexible and recognise your individual needs. *They enable you to study at your own pace and in local venues within the community.*

Change the typeface and/or pitch size for this paragraph only

Letters and memos

In this exam you are required to key in either a letter or a memo. The rules for such documents are the same as those given for text production in Section 2. The differences to look out for in the word processing exam are as follows.

- There are only a few editing instructions and you will not be required to correct word errors.
- You may be told to copy part of a previously stored document into your file.
- You may be asked to find missing items of information from a previous document and insert them into your file.
- You may be instructed to add some information from the Resource Sheet.
- You will be required to take extra copies of the document and show the routing.

Copies and routing

You are asked to provide two extra copies of the letter or memo and show the destination and routing on each copy. The quickest way is to key in the details at the bottom of your original document, as shown below, so that any copies you print out will contain that information. Routing can then be done on individual copies by ticking with a pen (not pencil) or by using highlighter. Alternatively, you may prefer to use the tick symbol, embolden or highlight the relevant name on the screen before printing off each extra copy. It is not essential for the details to appear on the original copy (blind copy).

Original	**1st copy**	**2nd copy**

Copy Sue Carfrae
        File
	Copy Sue Carfrae ✓
	        File
		Copy Sue Carfrae
		        File ✓

The following exercises will give you extra practice in the above features before you attempt a full practice exam.

Exercise 3.7

Key in this exercise using a memo heading from the CD–ROM. The memo is from Lucy Rose to Dillon Jacks Ref LR/Staff/73. The 2 items of information you need to add can be found in Exercise 3.5 (in this section). Remember to take 2 extra copies and show the destination and routing. Print a copy and check it with the worked example on page 140.

We talked about doing something different for our team outing this coming summer.

I have received a flyer from a local firm that offers Thames sailing barges for charter, and think this might appeal to everyone.

We could hire a barge for the day and take a trip up the River S____, embarking and disembarking in Whitstable harbour, and then book an early evening meal at the "Lobster Quadrille" on the quayside.

To keep costs down, Usama could be asked to provide drinks and a cold buffet lunch for us to eat onboard.

If you think this is worth looking into, the barge company would be happy to show us around one of their vessels before we make a booking. We can ring them on (add the telephone number here) for further details.

Top + 2 please. One for Usama Hussain and one for file. Indicate routing.

Exercise 3.8

Key in this exercise using a letterhead from the CD-ROM. The letter is to Mr Fin Witag 8 High Street KINGUSSIE PH21 1HX Our ref GS/NB/728196. The document you need for the extra paragraph is stored as ACT on the CD. Print a copy of your finished document and check it with the worked example on page 141.

Dear Mr Witag

There has never been a better time to apply for a Zenith Gold Card.

If you apply for your card before 1st April you will pay no interest on all purchases and balance transfers for the first 6 months.

After that, we offer a low long term rate of just 13.5% (APR variable) on all purchases. You can take advantage of interest free credit for up to 55 days if you clear your balance in full every month. Alternatively you can make a monthly payment of 2% of the outstanding balance.

There is no annual fee to pay and you can transfer all of your existing store and credit card balances to our Gold Card, thus saving yourself time and money. With a credit limit tailored to your requirements, you will benefit from increased spending power whenever you need it.

To take advantage of these benefits, simply complete the enclosed application form and return it to us without delay.

(Copy the 2nd paragraph from the document stored as ACT and insert here)

We look forward to being of service to you.

Yours sincerely

Guo Lishan
Marketing

Enc

(Top + 2 please. One for Mark Goodyer and one for file. Indicate routing.)

Exercise 3.9

Key in this exercise using a letterhead from the CD–ROM. The letter is to Mrs Olga Djokanovic 34 Hill Green LAVENHAM Suffolk CO10 5FG Our ref GPH/Client.875234. You will need to add some information from the Resource Sheet on page 57, supplied as part of this exercise. Remember to key just the details that are required. Print a copy of your finished document and check it with the worked example on page 142

Dear Mrs Djokanovic

As one of our healthcare policyholders, you will have received issues of our quarterly magazine. However, this is a very special edition of Wellwise, which marks the launch of a new service for our individual private medical insurance customers.

It is an online service called Health Watch and it is available only through the Internet. It is aimed at helping you and your family maintain your health and is an extension of our existing helpline telephone service.

In this issue of Wellwise, we explain exactly how Health Watch works. We describe in detail the structure and medical expertise behind the setting up of the service. You will discover how the symptom synopsis, medical dictionary, helpline and planner can give you confidence and reassurance.

To access Health Watch (add the instructions from the Resource Sheet here) and complete the registration form.

Wellwise also has fascinating articles about such wide ranging subjects as claims made for various popular diets to the arguments about immunising young children. There is an amusing commentary about the use of red wine versus white wine, for medicinal purposes only, of course!

Visit us at Health Watch today and enjoy the peace of mind that our professional expertise can bring to your home.

Yours sincerely

Clem Burke
Manager

Top + 2 please. One for Alex Blackman and one for file. Indicate routing.

RESOURCE SHEET

From: blackman.a@wellwise.com
Date: 28 June 2004
To: burke.c@wellwise.com
Subject: Health Watch Access

Clem

I promised to get back to you with the information you required. The instructions that need to go in the letters to our existing medical insurance customers are as follows (I've given you the correct personal code for Mrs Olga Djokanovic):

To access Health Watch visit www.HealthWatch.co.uk, select <u>New User</u> and enter your personal code: HW6752D56pmi and complete the registration form.

Hope you are happy with this. Once you have drafted the first letter I'll make sure the rest are sent out in time to meet the deadline.

Alex

Tables

You will have had practice already in producing complex ruled tables with sub-divisions and multiple headings and will have acquired most of the skills you need to work the Word Processing Level 3 exam table. However, there are a few differences.

- You will need to key the table in landscape format (longest sides at top and bottom).
- The table is divided into two sections, each with a different number of columns.
- Extra text to complete the table has to be taken from information supplied in a Resource Sheet.

Keying in and alignment

To work in landscape format, make sure you are in **Print Layout View**, then use **File→Page Setup→Paper Size**. The dialogue box looks like this.

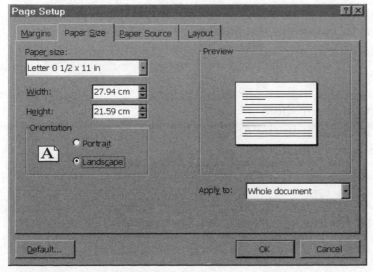

Figure 3.5 Formatting a table

From the *Orientation* box select **Landscape** and make sure that **Whole Document** is selected alongside *Apply To,* click **OK**.

Your ruler line now shows that your line length for keying in has increased to 24 cm, which means you cannot see the full width of the page, but you can use the arrows on the bottom scroll bar to move from left to right. You should still key in across each horizontal line of words, using the tab key or mouse to reach each column or cell. Inserting extra linespacing or altering column widths can be done once you have keyed in all the text. Before you do such editing, you may like to reduce the size of the table to fit your screen by selecting **50%** from the **Zoom** tab on the toolbar. This will give you a clear picture of the overall layout, although the individual words will be harder to read.

You should block all column headings and text to the left. Whole numbers and figures may also be blocked to the left, but in sums of money and measurements *decimal points must always be aligned.*

Column width and spacing between

Use **Table→Insert→Table** and select the number of columns you need for the first section of the table, click **OK**. You can easily create more rows as you go along by making sure your cursor is in the last cell on the right, and pressing the tab key. You can alter the width of any column by dragging the gridline to create the size you require. The column widths do not have to be the same and neither do the spaces between the columns.

Altering number of columns

Once you have completed the first section of the tab, create a new row, mark it and use **Table→Merge Cells** to allow you to key in the new main heading. Create another new row and use **Table→Split Cells** and select the number you need to allow you to complete the second section of the tab. You can drag the gridlines of the new columns to alter their widths without affecting those in the first section of the tab.

Resource sheet

In the exam the table is drafted with only part of the text filled in. You need to refer to the tear-off Resource Sheet that is at the back of the exam question paper. It will give you the information you need to complete the document. Not all of the information on the sheet will be required, nor will it be in the same order as in the draft table. You must be careful to

- extract only the information needed for the draft table
- key the information in the order shown in the draft table
- key the information under the correct headings.

Capitals

It is important that you follow copy regarding use of capitals in headings and listed items, or you could lose marks.

Ruling

You must follow the copy *exactly* regarding ruling of the table, or you will lose marks. Make sure you leave at least one character space either side of each column gridline. If you need to add or delete ruling, use the **Outside Borders** icons to select the formatting you need. You can drag the set of icons from the toolbar onto your screen if you wish to make it easier to access them.

Figure 3.6 Borders icons

Linespacing

The table in the exam is designed to fit onto one sheet of landscape A4 paper, but it can sometimes be a tight squeeze. If there is room to leave a clear linespace before and after each line of ruling, do so, as the finished document looks clearer and is easier to read. However, you will not be penalised in this exam if you are unable to leave such spacing.

The following exercises and accompanying Resource Sheets will give you extra practice in the above features before you attempt a full practice exam.

Exercise 3.10

Key in this exercise following the layout and ruling shown. Save your work frequently, to avoid losing it if you make an error. Remember to key in all text before adding linespacing or altering column widths. Print a copy with the longer edge at the top. Check it with the worked example on page 143.

ZENITH BANK PLC

DEPOSIT	WITHDRAWAL	INTEREST
Cash	Available immediately	Commences from next working day
Cheque deposited to account with cash card only	Available after 5 working days	Commences after 3 working days
Automated credits	Available immediately	Commences from next working day

FEES AND CHARGES

TYPE	INTEREST EAR %	MONTHLY RATE %	FEE £
Agreed overdraft	6.75	0.55	-
Unauthorised overdraft	19.09	1.52	12.00
Unpaid items due to insufficient funds	-	-	27.50 per item
Special clearance for cheques	-	-	15.00 per item
Deposit of foreign currency cheque	-	-	5.00 per item

Exercise 3.11

Key in this exercise following the layout and ruling shown. You will need to add some information from the Resource Sheet supplied for this (see page 63) and the next exercise. Print a copy with the longer edge at the top. Check it with the worked example on page 144.

SPRING SATURDAY SPECIALS 2004

COURSES ON CAMPUS

CODE	SUBJECT	DATE AND TIME	FEE £
SS1	Violent times - domestic and international politics	10 April, 1000-1600 hrs	15.75
SS2	Digital photography workshop	17 April, 1000-1630 hrs	25.00, covers materials

Refer to the Resource Sheet and abstract text for codes SS3-SS5 to complete the table. Follow the layout given here.

COURSES OFF CAMPUS

VENUE	SUBJECT	CODE	DATE	TIME	FEE £
The Pinetum	Identifying birdsong	SSV1	3 April	0700-1000 hrs	9.50
Black Friars' Abbey	Black Friars' dig revisited	SSV2	8 May	1100-1530 hrs	15.00
North Reach Docks	Maritime history	SSV3	15 May	1000-1600 hrs	18.50

Exercise 3.12

Key in this exercise following the layout and ruling shown. Allow the text in the first and last columns to wrap round the column space you have allowed. You will need to check an item and add some information from the Resource Sheet supplied for this (see page 63). Print a copy with the longer edge at the top. Check it with the worked example on page 145.

Centre this heading → **ARTS FESTIVAL**

GROUP MIME

TYPE	CLASS	AGE	TIME (MINS)	FEE £	NOTE
Groups comprised of at least 2 members and no more than 4 members	109	11 years and under	4	9.00 *(Please check this amount and amend if necessary)*	In all mime classes music and limited costumes and props may be used. Check detailed rules with organisers beforehand.
	110	12-14 years	4	9.00	

Refer to the Resource Sheet and abstract text to complete the Group Mime Section. Follow the layout given here.

CHORAL VERSE SPEAKING

CLASS	AGE	TIME (MINS)	FEE £	DESCRIPTION
225	11 years and under	5	9.00	Comprising any poem or rhyme, spoken as a group, with limited actions. No music, costumes or props allowed.
226	12-14 years	5	10.50	

RESOURCE SHEET

DAY SCHOOL PROGRAMME SPRING 2004

DATE AND TIME	CODE	SUBJECT	TUTOR	FEE £
10 April, 1000 - 1600 hrs	SS1	Violent times - domestic and international politics	M Parker	15.75
17 April, 1000 - 1630 hrs	SS2	Digital photography workshop	B Rogers	25.00, covers materials
8 May, 1000 - 1600 hrs	SS3	Architecture from Baroque to Palladian	D Koronka	15.75
15 May, 1100 - 1600 hrs	SS4	Present your facts with PowerPoint	L Dakin	20.50, covers floppy disk and handouts
22 May, 1800 - 2130 hrs	SS5	History of British wines	B Miles	30.00, includes buffet and wine tasting
29 May, 1000 - 1630 hrs	SS6	Creative writing - from imagination to paper	W Korda	15.75
29 May, 1000 - 1630 hrs	SS7	Looking at paintings in depth	S Morley	15.75

ARTS FESTIVAL - CHILDREN'S CLASSES

GROUP MIME

CLASS	TYPE	AGE	TIME (MINS)	FEE £	NOTE
109	Groups comprised of at least 2 members and no more than 4 members	11 years and under	4	8.50	In all mime classes music and limited costumes and props may be used. Check detailed rules with organisers beforehand.
110		12-14 years	4	9.00	
111		15-17 years	4	9.00	
112	Groups comprised of at least 5 members and no more than 15 members	11 years and under	8	15.00	
113		12-14 years	8	15.00	
114		15-17 years	10	17.50	

PUBLIC SPEAKING

CLASS	TYPE	AGE	TIME (MINS)	FEE £	NOTE
152		15 years and under	4	5.00	You may bring an object to talk about and refer to notes, but must not read a prepared speech.
153		16-17 years	4	5.00	
154		Open	4	7.00	

Section 4

Exam work

Common errors to avoid

Before you start a practice exam, you may like to compare documents from a past OCR exam question paper with the incorrect worked examples (see pages 65–79). Use your proofreading skills to see if you can identify the errors and then check how best to avoid them from the comments that follow.

Sample exam question paper – Document 1

DOCUMENT 1

2

Recall this document stored under _____ and amend as shown. Adjust margins to give a line length of 15 cm. Change to double linespacing (except where indicated) and use full justification. Insert and delete page breaks so that the document prints on 4 pages. Save as _____ and print one copy.

Progress College is a subsidiary company dedicated to ~~providing~~ *improving* learning and training opportunities for everyone.

within the Progress Group and is

OUR HOME STUDY SCHEME OFFERS YOU THE CHANCE TO LEARN AND DEVELOP SKILLS WITHOUT HAVING TO ATTEND A COLLEGE OR TRAINING CENTRE AT FIXED TIMES EACH WEEK.

Change this paragraph to lower case

✳ Inset this paragraph 25 mm from both left and right margins

been offering home study

Although our company has ~~only designed distance learning courses~~ for a relatively short time, Progress Group is well known and respected *in the field of education and training*. // We have a research and development section whose work includes market research to discover people's needs.

A series of pilot schemes is used as a monitor of success.

△ Page 2 starts here

people who are not working

We operate a special study discount for ~~all those who are unemployed~~, people receiving state support, ~~income support, family credit~~ or who have retired. // Please contact our student advisors on 01793 477488. They will be able to give you precise details of the available discounts.

those who may be disabled

Studying with Progress College means that you can:

Leave a space here at least 35 mm across from left margin by 40 mm down but no more than 45 mm across by 50 mm down. DO NOT RULE BOX.

start at any time of year
develop at your own pace
study at home or wherever is best for you
choose from a wide range of courses
gain the qualifications you need.

This section of text only in single linespacing

Please insert HOME STUDY as a header and May 1999 as a footer. Header and footer to appear on every page.

3

We are now able to offer ~~computing and~~ ~~word or~~ text processing. Some new caring and counselling courses are at present being developed.

More information will be available concerning these in the summer.

(Page 3 starts here)

at the present time

Details of the subjects available/are listed below ~~with more to follow~~.

Leisure and interests
Arts and general studies
Career and business skills
Counselling
Child care
Degrees and higher education
Publishing and writing
Developing your skills

(Sort into exact alphabetical order)

All our course materials are fully up to date and designed to be clear/so *and easy to follow* you can enjoy working through your chosen course.

Your pack will include everything you need; *study materials, details on how to contact your tutor, information on each module's aims and objectives and all the assignments you need to complete. These will be marked and returned to you by your tutor. The pack is accompanied by an explanatory video.*

(Move this paragraph to point marked △)

It is an ideal solution if you have work or family commitments, cannot find a class or you want to study at your own pace. With Progress College, you study for the same qualifications and take the same examinations as other students. You will also have a good chance of success.

(Page 4 starts here)

We also provide a timetable to help you plan your studying. *This will be designed to work round your other commitments. Your tutor will be happy to provide any further advice you may need.*

Please note that your fee includes free career advice, up to three years' study and full tutorial guidance and support while you are studying.

(Copy this paragraph to point marked ✳)

(Please change Progress College to Progress Learning throughout this document)

Document 1 – Worked example containing errors

See how many errors you can spot. Circle them and then check with the following list.

HOME STUDY   1

Progress Learning is a subsidiary company within the Progress Group and is dedicated to providing learning and training opportunities for everyone.

Our home study scheme offers you the chance to learn and develop skills without having to attend a college or training centre at fixed times each week.

Please note that your fee includes free career advice, up to three years' study and full tutorial guidance and support while you are studying.

Although our company has been offering home study courses for a relatively short time, Progress Group is well known and respected in the field of education and training.

We have a research and development section whose work includes market research to discover people's needs. A series of pilot schemes is used as a monitor of success.

It is an ideal solution if you have work or family commitments, cannot find a class or you want to study at your own pace. With Progress College, you study for the same qualifications and take the same examinations as other students. You will also have a good chance of success.

We operate a special study discount for all those who are unemployed, people receiving state support, those who may be disabled or who have retired. Please contact our student advisors on 01793 477488. They will be able to give you precise details of the available discounts.

Studying with Progress Learning means that you can:

start at any time of year
study at home or wherever is best for you
choose from a wide range of courses
gain the qualifications you need.

We are now able to offer computing and text processing. Some new caring and counselling courses are at present being developed. More information concerning these will be available in the summer.

Details of the subjects available at the present time are listed below with more to follow.

Arts and general studies

Career and business skills

Counselling

Child care

Degrees and higher education

Leisure and interests

Publishing and writing

All our course materials are fully up to date and designed to be clear and easy to follow so you can enjoy working through your chosen course.

Your pack will include every thing you need; how to contact your tutor, information on each odule's aims and objectives and all the assignments you need to complete. These will be marked and returned to you by your tutor. The pack is accompanied by an explanatory video.

We also provide a timetable to help you plan your studying. This will be designed to work roud your other commitments. Your tutor will be happy to provide any further advice you may need.

Document 1 – Comments

ERROR	COMMENT
4th para: text not inset	tick completed amendments, re-check at end
4th para: *courses* not deleted	check recall text deletions carefully
6th para: *College* should be *Learning*	use *Find and Replace* to change words, or you may miss one
page breaks not inserted	press *Control + Enter* to create each permanent hard page break
7th para: deletion not made	check recall text deletions carefully
7th para: new paragraph not started	tick completed amendments, re-check at end
footer not inserted	set both your header and footer at the start of the document
8th para: line of text omitted from list	when transposing text remember to *Paste* text into new position
9th para: faulty linespacing	make sure linespacing is altered for the bracketed text only
10th para: deletion not made	check recall text deletions carefully
10th para: list not sorted, line missing	use automatic *Table→Sort*, otherwise errors can creep in
11th/13th paras: faulty linespacing	use ¶ icon to show up inconsistent linespacing between paragraphs
12th para: *every thing* not closed up	check recall text amendments carefully, some are easily missed
12th para: text omitted	check that you have added all the extra handwritten text
12th para: *odule's* should be *module's*	proofread carefully to pick up any keying in errors
13th para: *roud* should be *round*	proofread carefully to pick up any keying in errors
14th para: paragraph moved instead of copied	copied text must appear **twice** in the document: use *Copy* and *Paste* moved text only appears **once** in the document: use *Cut* and *Paste*

Sample exam question paper – Document 2

DOCUMENT 2   4

Letter – Top + 2 please. One for Diane Sweet and one for file. Indicate routing. –

Our ref DV/en

Mr Lawrence Freeman
22 London Road North
Swatton Fields
BATH
BA1 6TB

Dear Mr Freeman

<u>Guide to Courses</u>

Thank you for your letter concerning our home study courses. I am arranging for our prospectus, which lists all the subjects we offer, to be sent to you today by separate post. The prospectus also gives information on how the courses are organised, together with details of our fees.

Copy first paragraph of document stored as INFORM and insert here

We strongly advise you not to send cash to us by post, not even by special delivery or a private courier. If you prefer you may telephone our student advisors who will be very happy to help you with any queries. If you would like to pay by credit or debit card our staff will take the details over the telephone. <u>Please have your card to hand to pay by this method</u>. For information on payment by instalments please read page 4 of our prospectus.

The fee includes all materials (which are yours to keep) and tuition for up to 3 years from the date of your enrolment.

We hope you are successful in your chosen career and we look forward to hearing from you.

Yours sincerely

Dominique Venison
Director

Document 2 – Worked example containing errors

See how many errors you can spot. Circle them and then check with the following list.

You can assume that the second paragraph has been correctly copied from the stored document.

PROGRESS GROUP

Progress House Westwood Way Coventry CV4 8JQ Telephone 024 76 470033

Our ref DV/en

Mr Lawrence Freeman
22 London Road North
Swatton Fields
Bath
BAJ 6TB

Dear Mr Freeman

Guide to Courses

Thank you for your letter concerning our hoe study courses. I am arranging for our prospectus, which lists all the subjects we offer, to be sent to you today by separate post. The prospectus also gives information on how the courses are organised, together with details or our fees.

Our company is able to help everyone by offering special discounts as well as payment by instalments. You may pay for the course you choose in full if you wish and we offer a discount of 15% for payment in full on enrolment. This may be by cheque or postal orders.

We strongly advise you not to send cash to us by post, not even by special delivery or a private courier. If you prefer you may telephone our student advisors who will be very happy to help you with any queries. If you would like to pay by credit or debit card our staff will take the details over the telephone. Please have your card to hand to pay by this method. For information on payment by instalments please read page 4 of our prospectus.

The fee includes all materials (which are yours to keep) and tuition for up to 3 years from the date of your enrolment.

We hope you are successful in your chosen career and we look forward to hearing from you.

Yours Sincerely

Dominique Venison
Director

enc

Copy to Diane Sweet

Document 2 – Comments

ERROR	COMMENT
date omitted	write a reminder on the top of the question paper
postal town in lower case	should always be in capitals: follow copy for capitalisation
1st para: *hoe* should be *home*	proofread carefully to pick up any keying in errors
1st para: *or* should be *of*	important to proofread: spellcheck will not highlight *or*
3rd para: faulty underscore	avoid marking the spaces before/after text for underscoring
4th para: faulty spacing	always key brackets close up to the text they belong to
complimentary close: faulty capital	sincerely/faithfully are always lower case when used as here
routing and extra copy missing	write a reminder at the bottom of the question paper: to show routing you may tick in ink against the name on one copy

Sample exam question paper – Document 3

DOCUMENT 3   5

Recall this document stored under   *and amend as shown.*
Display the whole document in 2 columns (newspaper style).
Save as   *and print one copy.*

PROGRESS LEARNING

Progress Learning is a subsidiary of Progress Group and was formed 6 months ago.

All existing courses, which demand attendance by students at set times, will still be available.

However Progress Learning ~~offers~~ courses by distance learning, which is a modern term for home study and which enables students to learn where and when it suits them.

Some pilot studies have been completed and have been extremely successful. Our staff have used their expertise to create course materials of a very high quality.

Change typeface and/or pitch size for this paragraph only

who have completed pilot courses

Students have said that they were able to fit their studies easily around working hours ~~(although some employers were not very helpful)~~ and domestic arrangements.

Parveen Akhtar enrolled on the Publishing and Writing course. She said, "My tutor has been the best. He has helped me enormously. I am so thrilled to have gained a distinction. I thoroughly enjoyed the course. This has certainly given me a boost; *I am hoping to start work soon."*

We like to give a personal service so we ensure that each student is allocated an individual tutor.

One successful student, Andrew Longworth, said "I am approaching 50 and have not studied anything since I left school at 15. I set aside an hour for study every day. In the winter I mostly studied in the evenings after work. *In the summer I enjoyed studying in the early morning. This new system of learning is brilliant."*

Student advisors may be contacted by telephone on 01793   4___.

You can write to Progress Learning at Woodpecker Mews, SWINDON, SN2 3PQ.
Their fax number is 01793 471184 and their E-mail address is (Please insert their E-mail address from the Resource Sheet).

Document 3 – Worked example containing errors

See how many errors you can spot. Circle them and then check with the following list.

The Resource Sheet, which you will need to refer to, is printed after the question paper for document 4.

PROGRESS LEARNING

Progress Learning is a subsidiary of Progress Group and was formed 6 months ago.

All existing courses, which demand attendance by students at set times, will still be available.

However Progress Learning offers courses by distance learning, which is a modern term for home study and which enables students to learn where and when it suits them.

Some pilot studies have been completed and have been extremely successful. Our staff have used their experience to create course materials of a very high quality.

Students who have completed pilot courses have said that they were able to fit their studies easily around working hours (although some employers were not very helpful) and domestic arrangements.

One successful student, Andrew Longworth, said "I am approaching 50 and have not studied anything since I left school at 15. I set aside an hour for study every day. In the winter I mostly studied in the evenings after work. In the Summer, I enjoyed studying in the early mornings. This new system of learning is brilliant.'

Parveen Akhtar enrolled on the Publishing and Writing course. She said, "My tutor has been the best. He has helped me enormously. I am so thrilled to have gained a distinction. I thoroughly enjoyed the course. This has certainly given me a boost; I am hoping to start work soon."

We like to give a personal service so we ensure that each student is allocated an individual tutor.

Student advisors may be contacted by telephone on 01793 471184

You can write to Progress Learning at Woodpecker Mews, SWINDON, SN2 3PQ. Their fax number is 01793 471184 and their E-mail address is pg@learn.co.uk.

– Worked example containing errors

rors you can spot. Circle them and then check with the following

et, which you will need to refer to, is printed after the question
nt 4.

| | All the students in this course passed: 80% with distinction, 15 % with credit and 5% passed. There were no failures |
| These results were no so good; 65% gained distinction, 2% passed with credit, 10% passed, but 7% failed. |

COURSES	CODES	TOPICS	TUTORS	COST £
		Desktop Publishing		
		Technical Writing		
		Editing Skills		
		Creative Writing		
		How to Draw Cartoons		
Supervisory and Management Skills		Effective Management of Time		
		Assertiveness		
		Management of stress		
		Supervisory Skills		

DETAILS OF OTHER HOME STUDY

COURSES	CODES	TOPICS	TUTORS	COST £
Basic Computing	Spreadsheets	IT100	Suzanna Ferguson	40.75
	Databases			36.50
	Communications			102.00
	Multimedia			146.25
Basic Word Processing	Keyboarding	IT200	Peter Winterburne	28.75
	Typing Conventions			17.65
	Document Design			15.80
	Saving Text			12.90
	Printers and Printing			25.50
	Disk Management			15.90

An alternative easy payment scheme is also available

Document 3 – Comments

ERROR	COMMENT
para 4: *experience* should be *expertise*	important to proofread: spellcheck will not highlight proper word
para 5: deletion not made	check recall text deletions carefully
para 6: faulty capital	summer does not have an initial capital: follow copy for capitals
para 6: *mornings* should be *morning*	important to proofread: spellcheck will not highlight proper word
para 6: single quote in final sentence	either double or single quotes may be used but must be consistent
para 7: transposition incorrect	interim text misplaced: write order on question paper as guideline
para 7: faulty linespacing	check linespacing between paragraphs after doing a transposition
para 9: *471184* should be *477488*	phone number found in document 1: fax number given in error

Sample exam question paper – Document 4

DOCUMENT 4

(Please key in as shown. Save as .... and print one copy with longer edge at the top. Rule as shown.)

DISTANCE LEARNING ◄── *(Centre this heading)*

6

COURSES	TOPICS	RESULTS
Publicity and Writing *(Please check this name and amend if necessary)*	Desktop Publishing, Technical Writing	*All the students in this course passed; 80% with distinction,* *(Refer to the Resource Sheet and abstract text required to complete this course and the Supervisory and Management Skills course only.)*

DETAILS OF OTHER HOME STUDY COURSES

COURSES	TOPICS	CODES	TUTORS	COST £
Basic Computing	Spreadsheets, Databases, Communications, Multimedia	IT100	Suzanna Ferguson	40.75, 36.50, 102.00, 146.25
Basic Word Processing	Keyboarding, Typing Conventions, Document Design, Saving Text, Printers and Printing, Disk Management	IT200	Peter Winterburne	28.75, 17.65, 15.80, 12.90, 25.00, 15.90

(Please modify layout - key in the CODES column as second column.)

An alternative easy payment scheme is also available.

Resource sheet

RESO...

PROG...

Woodpecker M...

Fa...

E-ma...

Wel...

COURSES	TUTORS
Publishing and Writing	Lavinia Wilson
Supervisory and Management Skills	Patrick Edwards
Basic Business Skills	Amelia Brooks

Document 4

See how many e...
list.

The Resource Sh...
paper for docume...

RESULTS

TOPICS

DISTANCE LEARNING

COURSES
Publishing and Writing

Document 4 – Comments

ERROR	COMMENT
main heading not centred	tick completed amendments, re-check at end
part 1 col 2: *stress* should have initial capital	capitalisation in lists must be consistent: follow copy
part 1 col 3: inconsistent space in *15 %*	display must be consistent: proofread carefully
part 1 col 3: omitted fullstop after *failures*	follow copy for punctuation: proofread carefully
part 1 col 3: *no* should be *not*	important to proofread: spellcheck will not highlight *no*
part 1 col 3: *;* should be	follow copy: proofread carefully, some are easily misread
part 2 main heading: redundant vertical lines	use *Table→ Merge Cells*: proofread lines as well as text
part 2 cols 2 and 3: text not transposed	text must follow relevant heading: proofread carefully
part 2 col 5: blocked display of money	decimal points must be aligned in money and measurements
part 2 col 5: *25.50* should be *25.00*	always check figures especially carefully
final line: fullstop missing	follow copy for punctuation: proofread carefully

You will have realised from the typical errors made in the above documents that in an exam more penalties are incurred through candidates failing to spot their own keying in errors than for any other reason. You can dramatically reduce such penalties if you develop good proofreading skills.

Exam practice

In this section new practice material similar to OCR exam standard is provided as follows:

Text Production Level 3, Example 1, with Instructions to Invigilator
Text Production Level 3, Example 2, with Instructions to Invigilator
Word Processing Level 3, Example 1, with Resource Sheet
Word Processing Level 3, Example 2, with Resource Sheet

Letterheads and memo headings, for recall as templates, together with recall text for word processing units are available on the CD-ROM.

Printed versions of the headings are available in Section 6, should you prefer to use those.

Worked examples of all documents are given in Section 5 of this book.

Practising for the exam

Try to complete each practice paper in one session and under exam conditions. You are allowed $1^{1}/_{4}$ hours to complete each text production unit and $1^{3}/_{4}$ hours for each word processing unit. Do not refer to your textbook or ask for help or advice while you are doing your 'mock exam'. Avoid any talking or interruptions. If possible, ask someone to act as an invigilator to time you and dictate the information you need for each text production unit. As well as checking your own finished work with the worked example, it is helpful to get someone else to mark it for you, as they may pick up on errors that you have missed. This will all help to give you some idea of when you are ready to sit a real exam. To gain experience and confidence, as well as improving on your accuracy and speed, get as much practice as you can by working on past OCR exam papers.

When practising exam work, get into good habits by making sure that you do the following:

- Record your name, centre number and document number on each printout.
- Save your work frequently as you edit your document.
- Proofread and spellcheck each document from screen before printing, and also at the end of the exam from the printout.
- Have a dictionary handy to check spellings you are unsure of.
- Use consistent linespacing and display of headings within a document.
- Tick off instructions as you complete them, to reduce the risk of omitting any.
- Carry out a final check of each completed document to make sure you have not duplicated or omitted any text, as this could cause you to lose a lot of marks.

Text production practice exam 1

Instructions to invigilator

About 15–20 minutes after the start of the examination, announce the following for Document 3.

The renovation will take approximately five years to complete.

The missing lecture lunch topic is bricks and mortar.

Text production practice exam 1 – Document 1

DOCUMENT 1

Letter to Mrs S Youel Focus Youth Group 280 London Rd
KING'S LYNN Norfolk PE34 6RY Our ref GRM24/288
Please use the heading GROUP MEMBERSHIP

Your ref FY/SK/Social

Dr Mrs Youel

Welcome to the Country House Trust. We are delighted that you have decided to join our group scheme. As requested, we have pleasure in enclosing the 12 membership cards for you to distribute to your branches. We would remind you that, to obtain free access to our properties, it is necy for the group leader to produce a valid card at the start of any visit.
(emphasise this sentence)   any subscriptions or

Thank you for giving us permission to reclaim tax on / donations you make to the trust. Additional funds generated by this scheme are greatly apreciated by us. The extra ~~revenue~~ income enables us to extend our conservation work even ~~further and to invest in more properties.~~

The booklets in the enclosed welcome packs give info on the properties that belong to our trust. ~~There is~~ a programme of events , including concerts, lectures and guided walks.

There is also a full educational programme that gives students' an opp for research, historical role-play and many other enjoyable activities.

We hope that your org will gain (enjoyment) and (great benefit) from your membership during the coming yr. [We shall contact you shortly to arrange the proposed meeting.

Yrs sncly

Alex Gray
Customer Care Manager

We note your wish to be involved
~~These facilities will be of particular~~
in such activities.
~~interest to your group.~~

Text production practice exam 1 – Document 2

DOCUMENT 2

(Memo from Alex Gray to
Marcia Dobson
Ref AG/GRM24/288)

(Please mark this URGENT)

I have been ~~exchanging~~

I am attaching a copy of the correspondance/with Mrs Y_____.
She is the Focus Youth Groups' sec and is likely to be a very
useful contact. Her experiense with young people could prove
helpful when we devellop the historical role-play exercises
planned for next season. Please contact her without delay
to arrange a meeting to discus her members poss
involvement in such activities. I should also like to be there
and could make a lunchtime appt on any day during the
week starting Monday (give date for first Monday of next month).

Can you give me a progress reports on the restoration work
being undertaken at Holly Hatch House? Last time I
enquired, the Lyttleton Suite in the east quarter was
being refurbished. I am hoping that it is now complete, as
this accommodation, together with the servants' rooms on
the top floor, is planned to be used for educational activities.
We shall also need to check that the health and safety
regulations we already has in place will cover the change
of use. The reason why I am keen to get any such
problems sorted out now are to avoid any difficulties
such as we have had in the past.

(Please ask Angus to take responsibility
for this.)

Text production practice exam 1 – Document 3

DOCUMENT 3

Use double linespacing except where indicated

RECENT DEVELOPMENTS

HOLLY HATCH MANOR ← Centre this heading

One of our recent acquisitions, this 17th century manor is undergoing renovation, which will take approx _ years to complete. However, we are now about to open the house to the public. Some parts of the building will be subject to temp closure, but we gntee you will still find your visit worthwhile.

You willl have the chance to see some of the restoration work being carried out. Much of the repairs to curtains, furniture and fabrics will be carried out on site. The original foundry and workshops are able to deal with most of the metal and wood work repairs. The _ _ _ _ _ quarter is being refurbished and will form part of the accommodation to be utilised for educational activities.

Educational Programme

Although most of the structural work is now complete, we are about to embark upon phase 2, which is as follows

1	Cleaning silverware
2	Restoring and cleaning china
3	Cleaning and repair of fabrics and wall/hangings
5̶ A	Equipping the education block
6̶ B	Completing the new restaurant
4̶ B	Setting up new displays throughout the rooms

Inset this section of text 25mm from left margin

Programme of Work

We plan an exciting range of activities for groups from youth and adult clubs, schools and colleges. They will

Text production practice exam 1 – Document 3 (cont)

have the chance to take part in historical role-play based on the daily lives of household servants, from the butler to the lowly scullery maid. Courses will be held on fabric, furniture, glass and china renovation. A series of lecture lunches will cover topics as varied as _ _ _, 17th century cooking and Tudor England[1]. Many of the original archives of the house will be made available for studying on site. Copies of key historical documents and interactive computer programs relating to the era will also be set up for students.

Barn Restaurant

These paragraphs only in single linespacing

Our luxurious licensed restaurant, which is due to open in October, is situated behind the main house in a restored hammer-beam barn. With its exposed beams, it provides a magnificent setting for our haute cuisine[2]. You can be confident that wee shall live up to these claims for our cooking ~~which aims for the very best quality.~~

We aim to use local produce, including vegetables, salads and herbs form our kitchen garden. // For the first fortnight we shall open daily at lunchtime only. After that, we shall also be open for evening meals, apart from Sundays.

Morning and afternoon snacks will be served in the sun room and the loggia. Details regarding menus, prices and times will be sent to you shortly, or you can ring us on 01263 897009.

The menu will be changed according to the season.

[1] A social history of the times
[2] Cookery of a very high standard

Text production practice exam 1 – Document 3 (cont)

<u>Gardens and Estate</u>

Work began early on the gardens nearest the house. The walled vegetable beds are already productive, although the glasshouses all need attention. The pineapple pit will need to be restored by specialists in the longer t4erm.

The formal lawns surrounded with clipped hedges and topiary yew trees have been restored to their former glory. Most of the herbaceous borders have been rescued from the undergrowth and replanted ready for the coming season. The more modern rock garden with its water featurs and alpine plants is also in ful working order.

Some of the outlying parts of teh estate are still suffering from neglect. PLans are in hand to thin and tidy the coppices. Many of the boundary fences need replacing. One ambitious project is to restore the lake area and repair the fountain and waterfall, but this long term scheme will have to wait until phase 4.

The estate includes a working farm that boasts a large herd of Guernsey cows. As well as producing milk, cream and cheese, the farm provides the estate with its own free-range chickens and eggs. All these products will be used in the new restaurant.

Text production practice exam 2

Instructions to invigilator

About 15–20 minutes after the start of the examination, announce the following for Document 3.

The wine presses hold 4 tons each.

Precise measures of yeast and sugar are added to the wine.

Text production practice exam 2 – Document 1

DOCUMENT 1

Letter to Mr N McCrathie Forrester & Son 203 Lever Street BRACKNELL Berks RG12 6PQ Our ref MS/Prom.269 Please use the heading CHAMPAGNE TREAT

Please mark this PERSONAL

Your ref NMcC/PP

Dr Mr McCrathie

Next month we are holding a special wine tasting evening to promote an interesting range of champagnes.

In appreciation of your loyalty and the long association of our cos ~~As you have been good customers of ours for many years~~, we have pleasure in inviting you to the event Enclosed are 4 tickets for your personal use/. and the use of your coleagues

The tasting starts at 2000 hrs and will be ~~directed~~ ted by ✓ the head of our buying dept, Claudette Simone. A hot and cold finger buffet will be available thrughout the evening.

Prior to the tasting a short video, Champagne: From Grape to Glass, will be shown. This features Rheims and Epernay vineyards and the process the grapes undergo to transform them into a quality product.

emphasise this sentence only

You may wish to take the opp to order cases of the various champagnes featured during the event. They will be ~~offered~~ ✓only to those attending this occasion.

We do hope that you will be able to attend what we are sure will prove to be a sucessful and enjoyable evening.

, at very attractive bargain prices,

Yrs sncly

Marius Shaw
Promotions Manager

Text production practice exam 2 – Document 2

DOCUMENT 2

Memo from Marius Shaw to Cass Martin
Ref MS/Prom. 270

I trust the arrangements for next month's wine tasting
is well in hand. [Please make sure that the Highlander
Hotel provides us with a suitable room in which to show
the video — — — — —.]
The room should seat up to 200 people and be close to the conference hall.

, who is directing the tasting,
Claudette S—— I have asked for the main hall to be laid out
with round tables each seating 10. A long tables is to be
provided on the dais. It might be politic to contact
Claudettes' sec to see whether she has any other special
requirements or instructions for us.

I am attaching a draft article with info that our guests
may find interesting. please send a fair copy of this
to the printers without delay. They gntee to include it
in the tasting cat as long as they receive it by Fri
(give date for first Fri of next month). I have been working
on the advertising and publicity material and I think it
will provide a useful introduction to the proceedings if
inserted before the listings' and tasting notes.

Please keep me informed of any problems that may
arise. I am out of the office for the remainder of the
week but should like to meet up with you on my
return to discuss developments and finalise the
arrangements.

, which has not always
been reliable in the past,

Text production practice exam 2 – Document 3

DOCUMENT 3

Use double linespacing, except where indicated.

THE BEST BUBBLY

Styles are based on the variety of grape used. The dry, non-vintage champagnes are usually a blend off black and white grapes, whilst the vintage wine is made from one variety and in smaller amounts.

True champagne can come only from a strictly demarcated region in northern France. It is made in the traditional way *and mfrs are subject to very rigid controls.*

Method

, often on a part-time basis

Most of the vines are cultivated by local farmers/who sell their grapes to the big houses or to co-operatives. Some even make wine themselves or buy it back to label and sell as their own. This means that there is no limit to the number of brands on the market. *However, there are approx 20 houses with the best-known names and the widest distribution. Their size and wealth allows them to use expencive equipment, employ the most experianced staff and store their vintage as long as poss. Their products thus become the brand leaders.*

, once it has been processed,

Producers

~~splitting sound~~

Harvesting takes place, with great care to avoid ~~breaking whole~~ grapes and with split fruit rejected, as prematurely crushed grapes give colour to the juice. *If necy the crop is sorted by hand before passing into huge vertical presses, which hold — tons each. The pressing is repeated 3 or 4 times with the cake of skins and stalks being divided and redistributed each time. The first pressing is kept for the house blend and the remaining must is left to ferment*. If it is too acidic it is decanted into steel tanks that encourage a secondary fermentation.*

* *in aged oak barrels*

Text production practice exam 2 – Document 3 (cont)

2

The wine is racked to cleanse it several times during the winter months. In the spring it is tasted and sorted into lots for blending. It is then bottled and precise measures of _ _ _ are added. This causes fermentation to begin again too produce the fizz.

These paragraphs only in single linespacing

Storage

The wine is stored in cold, dark, lime stone cellars for between 2 and 5 years, depending on the vintage.

After sevral months the bottles are moved to special racks that enable them to be slightly shaken, twisted and tipped daily** until they stand vertically. This results in the yeast sediment collecting at the end of the cork. The bottle's necks are then passed through a freezing tank, the corks are removed and the pressure inside blows the frozen sediment out. The contents are immed topped up and mushroom corks wired into place.

The bottles are returned to the cellar to rest and be allowed to mature. They are then washed, labelled and embellished with the distinctive gold foil cover that is the hallmark of true champagne.

** for about 3 months

Text production practice exam 2 – Document 3 (cont)

3

Storing and Serving at Home

Think of champagne as just like any other wine, with styles to suit all types of occasions and accompany many different kinds of food. Most people cannot tell the difference betwen a modestly priced and an expensive vintage.

There are a few suggestions fro storing and serving: *(Centre this line only)*

(Inset this section of text 25mm from the left margin)

1   Keep new champagne for at least 3 months

2   Buy a bottle each month, drinking the oldest first

3   STore in a cold place - a cellar or old fridge in a garage

4   Cool for 20 minutes before serving in a bucket of half ice and half cold water

5   Allow 3 glasses per head for a p;arty but only half as much if served as an aperitif or used as a toast

8 6   Any trace of grease or detergent on a glass can affect the fizz

6 7   Remove the wire, cover the cork with a teatowel and ease off gently

7 8   To preserve the bubbles, pour slowly into a slightly tilted glass

This glorious drink should be enjoyed whenever the mood takes you and not reserved just for special occasions.

Word processing practice exam 1

Recall text for this practice examination is available on the CD-ROM. The filenames are given in the instructions on the relevant questions.

The Resource Sheet is printed on page 99.

Word processing practice exam 1 – Document 1

DOCUMENT 1

Recall this document stored under WP1 recall 1 and amend it as shown. Adjust margins to give a line length of 14 cm. Change to double linespacing (except where indicated) and use full justification. Insert and delete page breaks so that the document prints on 4 pages. Save as WP1 DOC1 and print one copy.

HOME ZONE PATROL ← *Centre this heading*

(A)

ABOUT THE COMPANY *Inset this paragraph 15mm from both left and right margins*

This internationally based company is managed by a team of executives who have gained experience from working in many different areas of the security sector. *Our managers have experience of providing services to residential communities throughout Europe.*

Each <del>of our local area offices</del> covers *a limited number of clients within* *control centre* a defined area. These centres are manned by local personnel who know the neighbour hood and its particular concerns. All such staff are carefully screened and either have police, emergency service or military backgrounds. <del>We follow the British standard code of practice.</del>

The company was started in Italy 8 years ago.

Move to (B)

We are proud to offer a supporting role to existing emergency services. Our clients have the peace of mind of knowing that we are able to respond immediately.

Page 2 starts here

EXTRA COVER

We offer the following facilities:

immediate response to alerts
response to third party calls
securing damaged property
second keyholder function
school patrols at arrival *and departure times*
first aid help
storage of clients' critical data
vehicle patrols pass properties every hour

sort into exact alphabetical order

Please insert COMMUNITY SAFETY as a header and INTRODUCTION as a footer. Header and footer to appear on every page.

WHAT WE COVER

guarantee

For an additional fee we <del>undertake</del> to carry out a check twice a day of premises where owners are on holiday or on long term postings

✓

Word processing practice exam 1 – Document 1 (cont)

abroad. Confirmation and duration of survey is logged and supplied to the owners by e-mail.

We can mount silent remote control panic alerts to the outside of your property. We also provide a digital and video record of valuables, which can be used to assist insurance claims.

Page 3 starts here

and they are required to attend refresher courses frequently

PATROL SYSTEM

Our vehicles are 4-wheel drive Combotrucks, thus allowing us to cope with all weather conditions. All vehicles are equipped with a full range of emergency equipment, including first aid and fire fighting apparatus.

This paragraph in single linespacing

All personnel have voice and data communication with their bases, including a satellite tracking and monitoring system. There are backup patrols in the event of multiple alerts.

Each vehicle services not more than 300 premises within its residential area. This ensures high quality maintenance and fast response times.

B

Page 4 starts here

SCREENING AND TRAINING

The training of our response personnel is rigorous. In addition to tuition on a wide range of security issues, they receive intensive training in advanced driving, crime scene protection, primary first aid and basic fire fighting.

All our staff are carefully checked through police ~~computer data~~ ~~central criminal~~ records. Only those with impeccable references and credentials are accepted for training. ✓

CHARGES

as a special introductory offer

The standard package is available/at a cost of under £5 per day. The rates for extra cover can be negotiated based on individual requirements.

Copy to A

Our company is proud to offer you a unique, valuable and reliable service.

Change alerts to alarms throughout this document

Word processing practice exam 1 – Document 2

DOCUMENT 2

> Letter to Mr D Arkell   The Grange
> Wildernesse Avenue   YORK YO3 5SJ
> Our ref GV/HZP/Promo

Dear Mr Arkell

We are pleased to announce that we have extended our operation to cover the city of York. You may have noticed our patrol vehicles in your locality during the past few weeks. We have been surveying the area prior to offering our service to a select number of clients.

Home Zone Patrol provides a unique emergency response service to client home owners. It ensures that immediate response is available 24 hours a day. Our special introductory offer is [Please add the details from the Resource Sheet].

> Leave a space here at least 35 mm across from left margin by 35mm down but no more than 45 mm across by 50 mm down. DO NOT RULE BOX.

Our patrols are manned by fully trained personnel. They drive past each client's home at least once an hour throughout the day and night. They will respond immediately to any alarm, regardless of severity, cause or frequency. Their brief is to provide a front line response to threat or harm caused by criminals, vandals, general disturbances, accidents or natural disasters.

In today's society, in which 1 out of 3 people are victims of crime at some stage in their lives, we aim to bring you and your family peace of mind. Although it is a fairly new concept in this country, the service we offer is a welcome and common facility in Europe and America.

You are one of the select home owners in York to whom we are making our initial approach. If you think that our service will be of benefit to you, we should be delighted to arrange an appointment at our offices or in your home. Just give us a ring at the number on our letterhead. We look forward to helping keep your community, your family and your home secure.

Yours sincerely

Guillio Vincente
Director UK Operations

> Top + 2 please. One for Digby Lyttleton and one for file. Indicate routing.

Word processing practice exam 1 – Document 3

DOCUMENT 3

Recall this document stored under WP1 recall 3 and amend as shown. Display the whole document in 2 columns (newspaper style). Save as WP1 DOC3 and print one copy.

FIRE FIGHTING

Change this sentence to lower case

IF A FIRE BREAKS OUT IN YOUR HOME, ALERT THE EMERGENCY SERVICES AND HOME ZONE. Our C — patrol vehicles can reach you quickly and carry extinguishers and basic equipment to deal with minor fires.

to help reduce injury and damage

In the meantime, there are some basic actions you should take. The most important thing is to get everyone out of the house. When following your escape route, if a door feels hot, do not open it. ~~Use another route such as a window.~~ Close doors and windows behind you, to reduce the spread of flames and fumes. Keep as near to the floor as possible. If you are above the ground floor, knot bedding or clothing together to form a rope. Use this to climb down as far as you can before jumping. If there is no safe way down, shut the door, open the window and shout for help.

and secure it to heavy furniture

Change the typeface and/or pitch size of this sentence only.

Do not attempt to tackle a fire yourself if it is fierce or spreading ~~or looks as if it could become so.~~ you should heed the following advice When using an extinguisher ~~a basic code should be followed.~~

Copy the last paragraph of the document stored as EXTINGUISHERS and insert here

Keep a level head and do not panic. Remember, help is on its way.

In your car you should install a 1.4 kg extinguisher containing either dry powder or vaporising liquid. Keep it secured beneath the dashboard or in the driver's footwell, but not in the boot. Ideally you should have it checked annually.

Word processing practice exam 1 – Document 4

DOCUMENT 4

Please key in as shown. Save as WP1 DOC 4 and print one copy with the longer edge at the top. Rule as shown.

YORK CONTROL CENTRE – STAFFING

KEY OFFICE BASED PERSONNEL

NAME	JOB TITLE	CONTACT NUMBER	ADDRESS
Guillio Vincent	Add Guillio's job title here	01904 647566	16 Holgate Road, York, YO2 6BN
Ernest Arnold	Centre Manager	01904 659009	33 Scarcroft Lane, York, YO1 9NB
Molly Longley	Control Co-ordinator	01904 622659	20 North Road, Bootham, YO3 6PY
Jack Dillon	Technical Supervisor	01756 793667	Low Farm, Skipton, BD23 76H
Nadia Porter	Operations Administrator	01751 431268	The Grange, Sinnington, YO6 7RT

Please check this name and amend if necessary.

PATROL PERSONNEL ROTA – WEEK 1

SECTOR	ROLE	NAME	SHIFT	RATE PER HOUR £
Alpha	Patrol Chief	Bernie Miles	Early	18.00

Refer to the Resource Sheet and extract the remaining relevant details from those given in the table. Please follow the layout given here.

Word processing practice exam 1 – Resource sheet

RESOURCE SHEET

From: lyttleton.d@homezone.com
Date: 14 April 2004
To: vincente.g@homezone.com
Subject: Introductory Offer

Guillio

You asked me to double-check the York special introductory offer, which is a weekly rate of £30 for our standard cover with the rate fixed for a full year.

Regards

Digby

PATROL PERSONNEL ROTA – WEEK 1

NAME	STAFF NUMBER	SECTOR	ROLE	SHIFT	RATE PER HOUR £
Maggie Henderson	PP02	Alpha	Driver	Early	14.50
Varun Bhadeshia	PP11	Beta	Patrol chief	Late	18.00
Denzil Peach	PP06	Beta	Driver and first-aider	Late	17.25
Paula Woods	PP04	Charlie	Patrol chief and paramedic	Night	24.75
Jason Kendall	PP13	Charlie	Driver	Night	16.00
Miles Trumper	PP15	All	Standby officer	Day (12 hours)	7.50
David Levy	PP09	All	Standby officer	Night (12 hours)	9.00

Word processing practice exam 2

Recall text for this practice examination is available on the CD-ROM. The filenames are given in the instructions on the relevant questions.

The Resource Sheet is printed on page 106.

Word processing practice exam 2 – Document 1

DOCUMENT 1

Recall this document stored under WP2 recall 1 and amend it as shown. Adjust margins to give a line length of 13 cm. Change to double linespacing (except where indicated) and use full justification. Insert and delete page breaks so that the document prints on 4 page. Save as WP2 DOC 2 and print one copy.

HINTS FOR DRIVERS AND PASSENGERS

TRAVELLING SAFELY

Please insert SECURITY as a header and MODERN MOTORING as a footer. Header and footer to appear on every page.

<u>Maintenance and Safety Checks</u>

Check all lights, replacing any bulbs that may have blown.

that is provided with your vehicle

Study the driver's handbook. The invaluable information it contains includes a step-by-step guide to the basic checks you should carry out to maintain your car safely.

, but definitely prior to long journeys,

Preferably each week check the levels of petrol, brake fluid, engine oil, coolant and windscreen wash. Clean the lights, front and rear windscreens, and ensure washers and wipers are working efficiently. Regularly carry out an inspection of the engine pipes, hoses and fluid reservoirs, looking for possible leakage. Make sure all tyres are kept at the correct pressure and that treads are within the statutory limits. *The handbook contains information about the correct pressures for front and rear tyres. It also recommends adjustments for different weather conditions.*

Copy to △

Regular servicing by a reputable garage is very important. The vehicle logbook lists the recommended services depending on the age of your car or the mileage.

Page 2 starts here

<u>Safety Appliances</u>

brands that fall into the following

There are many different categories:

adult seatbelt
dog safety belt
bucket seat
booster cushion
carrycot restraint
carrycot harness
child harness
estate car grilles

this list only in single linespacing

Sort into exact alphabetical order

Word processing practice exam 2 – Document 1 (cont)

<u>Birth to 9 Months</u>

Use a carry cot restraint with straps that ~~fasten~~ *secure* it to the rear seat. The harness should have a quick release buckle. ✓

Alternatively, a first size bucket seat can be fitted on the front or ~~the back~~ *rear passenger* seat, with the baby facing towards the rear. ✓

(Page 3 starts here)

<u>Over 5 Years</u>   (This makes them easy to adapt to different vehicles.)

A bucket seat fastened to the rear seat is suitable. Some models are secured with a diagonal seat belt. There must be a crotch strap to pass between the child's legs.

<u>Between 9 Months and 5 Years</u>

Either a child's harness or an adult safety belt with a special booster cushion can be used on a back seat.

<u>Protection Against Theft</u>   (Locking devices for handbrakes, steering-wheels and gear leavers are effective.)

Only the most expensive security systems will deter a professional thief. However, fairly simple ones will put off casual thieves and joy riders. ~~All can be fitted by the car owner~~ Another basic deterrent is to etch the windows with the registration number. This would put off a thief, as windows and number plates would need replacing.

Expensive electrical systems will either set off an alarm if doors are tampered with or immobilise the ignition system ~~should anyone unauthorised attempt to start the engine~~.

(Page 4 starts here)

(Move to ◉)

When buying a child's safety seat, first consider the age of the child. Bear in mind that he or she will grow. Whichever type of seat or harness you buy, make sure it complies with British Standard BS3254 or European Standard ECE44.

(Inset this paragraph 25mm from both left and right margins)

Expensive devices include push-button codes, ultrasonic sensors and voltage sensors. Such devices are often fitted as standard in top of the range vehicles, but are increasingly offered as options on moderately priced models.

△   (Change expensive to sophisticated throughout this document.)

Word processing practice exam 2 – Document 2

DOCUMENT 2

Recall this document stored under WP2 recall 2 and amend as shown. Display the whole document in 2 columns (newspaper style). Save as WP2 DOC2 and print one copy.

COPING WITH CAR ACCIDENTS

Should you be involved in
~~In the unfortunate event of~~ an accident, you <u>must stop immediately</u> if any person, other than yourself, has been injured.

If damage has been caused to another car or property, or a domestic animal, other than a cat, has been injured, you are also obliged to stop. Failing to do so is an offence involving a fine, endorsement on your licence and possible disqualification.

change the typeface and/or pitch size for this sentence only.

Copy the last 2 paragraphs of the document stored as OFFENCES and insert here.

To avoid more vehicles becoming involved, it is important to warn other traffic. Call the police if anyone is hurt or the road is blocked. Anyone badly hurt should be moved by medically qualified persons only.

injured
Once any ~~who may have been hurt~~ are receiving attention, take particulars and find witnesses. Record any evidence on the spot, either by drawing a diagram or taking photographs.   *Change this paragraph to upper case*

The risk of severe injuries to passengers can be reduced by taking sensible precautions. Seat belts should always be fastened. Babies and children should use suitable safety seats and harnesses. Make sure they comply with *Please add both standard names and numbers here.*

Many new cars come with airbags fitted or offered as optional extras. ~~These are normally provided just for front seats.~~ *Although they can work very efficiently to minimise injury, they can be dangerous to babies or young children. For that reason, such passengers should not travel in seats with airbags.*

Word processing practice exam 2 – Document 3

DOCUMENT 3

Please key in as shown. Save as WP2 Doc 3 and print one copy with the longer edge at the top. Rule as shown.

COURSES ON CAR MAINTENANCE AND SAFETY ← *Centre this heading*

Title	Content	Venue	Date	Time hrs	Session Fee £
Securing Your Vehicle	Fitting alarms, combination locks, window etching	City Polytechnic	6,13 Sept	1830	9.75

Refer to the Resource Sheet and extract the remaining relevant details from those given in the table. Please follow the layout given here.

COPING WITH ACCIDENTS

Content	Details	Date and Time
Responding to the incident, first aid, mending details, legal responsibilities and implications, insurance matters.	This one-day courses at the City Polytechnic, designed to help you deal with traffic accidents confidently and efficiently. The auto repair yard will be used to stage incidents. Theory will be taught in the adjoining classroom.	9 and 23 October from 1000 hrs to 1600 hrs

Word processing practice exam 2 – Document 4

DOCUMENT 4

Letter to Mrs P Dawson   68 Merstham Road REDHILL R111 4DC
Our ref CMCourses/HT2/35

Dear Mrs Dawson

I refer to your telephone call last month when you enquired about the short courses we were starting in the autumn on vehicle maintenance and safety. You were interested to know whether we were able to offer a course covering holiday travel. I understand that you and your family plan to drive across France to southern Spain, towing a caravan for the first time.

Please check this date and amend if necessary.

Our marketing team discovered that there was interest in such a course and that a local travel agent would be happy to sponsor and host two sessions. These will be held at M———Travel plc in Redhill on 20 and 26 November from 1000 hrs to 1600 hrs. Their staff training facilities can accommodate up to 20 delegates and their catering manager will provide *(Insert details from Resource Sheet)* for each session for an additional charge of £10 per head.

Leave a space here at least 45mm accross from left margin by 35mm down but no more than 60mm accross by 50mm down. DO NOT RULE BOX

You may also find that another course we are running in October would be of use to you. This gives practical advice about how to cope with accidents in this country and abroad. It helps you to ensure that your insurance arrangements are adequate. In view of the fact that this is your first journey abroad, towing your caravan, such a course would provide you with valuable information and help boost your confidence.

I am unable to let you know the fee for this course, as I am awaiting this information from the City Polytechnic, where the sessions will be held. These have proved extremely popular in the past. As soon as I have any further details I will contact you, so that you can make an early application, should you be interested.

Yours sincerely

Nick Parsons
Administrative Officer

Top + 2 please. One for Jim Tomlinson and one for file. Indicate routing.

Word processing practice exam 2 – Resource sheet

RESOURCE SHEET

COURSES ON CAR MAINTENANCE AND SAFETY

Title	Content	Code	Date	Time hrs	Venue	Session Fee £
Basic Maintenance	Checking fluids, tyres, lights, brakes etc	BM9	4, 11 Dec	1030	Reigate Polytechnic	9.75
Advanced Maintenance	Adjusting fan belt, flushing radiator, repairing dents	AM7	13, 20 Oct	1900	Reigate Polytechnic	15.50
Holiday Travelling	Towing, legal documents and requirements abroad, driving in snow, car hire, insurance	HT2	20, 27 Nov	1000	Mattheson's Travel plc, Redhill	17.00

FROM   Patrick Keohane
DATE   2 August 2004
TO   parsons.n@city.ac.uk
SUBJECT   Holiday Travelling Course

Hi Nick

This is just to confirm that for a charge of £10 per head our catering manager will provide morning coffee, a cold buffet lunch and afternoon tea and cake for the courses we are sponsoring for you in November. I will confirm other details nearer the time.

Cheers

Patrick

Section 5

Worked examples

This section provides worked examples of each of the exercises and practice exams in Sections 1–4.

Use your proofreading skills to check them carefully against your own work.

Remember that exam candidates incur more penalties through failing to spot their own keying-in errors than for any other reason.

Exercise 1.1

Our exciting new catalogue is now out. Choose from British hotel stays to foreign tours.

Our company inspectors check catering and accommodation to ensure it is of the high

standard our customers demand.

We recommend our star value holidays with full board, excursions and activities all

included in the price. We can guarantee that you will receive value for money. We also

offer a selection of special interest holidays, each hosted by an experienced tutor.

Exercise 1.2

The passengers in the back seat were alarmed as the car's speed increased.

I leave college in two weeks' time. It's amazing how time flies!

The hotel's jacuzzi accommodates 10. Each seat has its own control to alter the jet flow.

This company's director is also on two associated companies' boards, but it's all above board!

The children's toys are displayed in the store's window. The ladies' wear is located on the first floor.

Exercise 1.3

Run-Master Folding Treadmill

This updated treadmill features the 'Easy Fold' system, which allows it to be folded to half its size with minimal effort. The console offers 7 programmes, including heart rate control. Pulse rate monitoring is carried out via a wireless chest belt (included in the accessories).

The equipment is fully guaranteed with a lifetime cover on the frame and 10 years' cover on the motor. The treadmill weighs 91 kg and part of it needs assembling. There is a large LED display showing time, speed, distance and incline. It also calculates heart rate and calories used. There are 3 target, 3 pre-set and 2 heart rate control programmes.

The powered elevation range is 0 % to 15 %. The running surface is 132 cm x 45 cm and overall dimensions are 163 cm x 91 cm x 145 cm. The equipment is designed to be used by persons weighing no more than 120 kg (265 lb). The price for the complete package is £995.

Exercise 2.1

CENTURY BANKING PLC 140 George St EDINBURGH EH2 5PW
www.centurybank.com

(date of exercise)

Our ref IB/Intro/id

Your ref M72811

Mrs L Mackie
63 Atlantic Quay
GLASGOW
G2 9KD

Dear Mrs Mackie

INTERNET ACCESS

Our free Internet banking service makes life so much easier.

There is no need to open any new accounts. It is simply an alternative way of accessing your existing ones. Of course, you can still continue to contact us using traditional methods: by visiting or telephoning a branch.

You can check your recent transactions and up-to-date balance immediately, at the click of a mouse. This information is available at any time, day or night, for 365 days of the year. You can also pay bills and transfer money.

We can assure you that our levels of security are of the highest. We provide an Internet banking fraud guarantee. This ensures that, in the unlikely event of fraud, we will refund your money.

To register, go to www.centurybank.com/register and complete the short application form. Alternatively you can register at any of our branches. We enclose a leaflet giving further details of this service, including contact numbers and e-mail addresses.

We look forward to hearing from you and welcoming you online soon.

Yours sincerely

Iain Duncan
Technology Manager

Enc

Exercise 2.2

FitFun 273 Victoria Street LONDON SW1E 3MP
Tel/Fax 020 7730 2689 E-mail services@fitfun.com

(date of exercise)

Our ref   Cat04/JT/D450

Your ref   ED/MF

PERSONAL

Mrs E Dubois
Riverside Cottage
3 Silverton Lane
ROTHBURY
NE65 9NB

Dear Mrs Dubois

FITNESS FOR ALL

We are pleased to enclose our new fitness catalogue, which you requested last month. We apologise for the delay, due to printing problems, but are sure you will appreciate the quality of our firm's products and feel the inconvenience was worthwhile.

Our equipment, of the highest quality and value, is suitable for any level of fitness. A toned and healthy body is an achievable way to improve your self-esteem. Investing in the correct exercise equipment to use in your own home is an efficient way of utilising your time and avoiding expensive club fees.

Each item of equipment comes with full details for assembly, instructions for use and a recommended exercise programme. All parts are covered by our comprehensive company guarantee.

A separate order form is enclosed for mail order. Alternatively you may use our secure online service at www.fitfun.com. To find a product type, simply key the item code into the search box at the top of the page and click on 'go'. You will receive an e-mail acknowledging receipt of your order and giving you despatch information. In the unlikely event that you need to return any goods, details of how to do this are given on the despatch note.

Exercise 2.2 (cont)

2

We are confident that you will find the equipment to suit your requirements and look forward to being of service to you.

Yours sincerely

Jo Tuck
Marketing

Encs

Exercise 2.3

Bingham-Newland Travel
80 Milton Road PETERBOROUGH PE6 4SD
Tel: 0733 380653   www.bing-new.com   travel@bing-new.co.uk

(date of exercise)

Our ref PdeH/C5811

Your ref 72811

PRIORITY

Mr and Mrs Johnston
12 Market Square
FOLKESTONE
Kent
CT20 4PO

Dear Mr and Mrs Johnston

TEMPTING TRIPS

As it is some time since your last holiday with us, you might like some information on the new holidays our organisation has just introduced.

The foreign travel, which may appeal to you, includes destinations such as a tour through Borneo's rainforests and a journey across Bulgaria. We also offer new luxury cruises to South America and Greenland on board ships exclusively used by our company.

New special interest holidays feature in the enclosed catalogue, such as photography in Vietnam and modern jazz in Portugal.

Flights to most destinations can be booked through a choice of 15 regional airports. Accommodation is provided for single travellers at no extra cost.

We also enclose a leaflet advertising miscellaneous products and services available from our order department. These include insurance and travel accessories.

By completing and returning the questionnaire on the back page, you can ensure that you will receive details from us of only those items that are of interest to you. It will guarantee you entry into our prize draw, where you will have a chance to win £1,000 worth of vouchers to spend on your next holiday with us or on goods from the leaflet, if you prefer.

Exercise 2.3 (cont)

2

We look forward to hearing from you soon, as we are confident that you will find a holiday to tempt you.

Yours sincerely

Peta De Haan
Manager

Encs

Exercise 2.4

MEMORANDUM

FROM   Iain Duncan

TO   Judy Blum

REF   ID/IB62

DATE   (date of exercise)

I have just drafted the attached letter to a Mrs Mackie. I should like a similar letter sent out to each client on our database who does not currently hold an Internet account. You will need to ensure that we have sufficient leaflets to send out with this mail shot.

I am starting a staff training session on our new spreadsheet software on Wednesday (*you should have inserted here the date for the first Wednesday of next month*). Initially I am asking section heads to recommend a member of their team to attend this first session, which will run from 1000 hrs to 1200 hrs.

Further training will be arranged as necessary and I am asking all interested staff to contact you. Please start a list so that we can find out the demand. I am sure that staff trained in the first session will share their knowledge with colleagues in their sections, although I believe many people will prefer to be given the opportunity to take part in a formal training session.

Att

Exercise 2.5

Memorandum

From Jo Tuck

To Nan Moretti

Ref JT/MP.launch

Date (date of exercise)

FITNESS FOR ALL

I am pleased to confirm that the printing problems have been resolved and we are now able to send the new catalogue out. The address for ordering online is www.fitfun.com.

We are about to launch a sophisticated range of equipment, which has an amazing number of electronic features.

Attached for your information is a copy of the advertisement that will appear in the usual magazines and periodicals.

The official launch evening has been booked at Park Hotel for Friday (*you should have inserted here the date for the last Friday of next month*). I will ask your secretary to make an appointment for me to give you the usual briefing prior to the event.

I am out of the office tomorrow, attending the committee monitoring the safety aspects of fitness equipment. One of the items on the agenda is the effect of the new European Union legislation. Rest assured that I shall report back to you immediately with any findings or recommendations that may affect our business.

Att

Exercise 2.6

Bingham-Newland Travel

MEMO

To	Jamie Cullum
From	Peta De Haan
Ref	PdeH/Sm
Date	(date of exercise)

URGENT

I think the current leaflet advertising our travel products and services needs redrafting. I attach a copy for your information. The format looks rather uninteresting and would benefit from the addition of some colourful graphics.

I should prefer the draft on the prize draw, where clients have the chance to win £1,000, to be moved from its current back page position to the middle of the leaflet. This would improve the impact and it could be printed on a 'tear-out' page.

Could you work on a flyer that can be inserted in the updated leaflet? I should like the new special interest holidays featured in our catalogue, such as photography in Vietnam and modern jazz in Portugal, to be given star billing.

I should appreciate an opportunity to meet up next week to go through the advertising material needed for the trade fair in Birmingham in 2 months' time. I know that a great deal of work on these has already been completed by your team and I am looking forward to seeing the new material. Please ring Sally to fix a suitable date when we are both available.

Att

Exercise 2.7

ARTS FESTIVAL CONDITIONS

<u>Eligibility</u>

The competitions are intended for amateurs, but professionals may take part as conductors or accompanists.

Adjudicators may not judge a class in which any of their pupils are competing.

<u>Scheduling</u>

Entrants will be given at least 2 weeks' notice of the dates and times of competition classes. ***Entry fees will only be returned if a class is withdrawn.***

No entries will be accepted after Monday (*You should have inserted here the date for the last Monday of next month*) and no alterations to competitors' chosen pieces will be accepted after this date.

<u>Judging and Marking</u>

A high standard is expected from performers and our judges will mark accordingly. <u>Their decision is final</u>.

Any complaints should be made in writing to the festival secretary immediately after the performance.

Exercise 2.7 (cont)

2

Mark sheets and certificates may be obtained free of charge at the end of each class. All awards will be presented at the final concert. They are awarded in accordance with national standards[1] as follows:

1   Performance - 75%[2] (aged under 12)

2   Merit - 81%

3   Commended - 84%

4   Distinction - 87%

5   Honours - 90%

Permissions

An agreement has been reached with the appropriate body that permission is not necessary for the solo performance of poetry or prose lasting no longer than 10 minutes.

Group drama is not covered by this agreement and it is up to the performers to obtain the relevant permits before submitting entries.

Amateur scripts or pieces of music are not affected, so no official permission needs to be sought other than an acknowledgement to the author or composer.

Copyright

The festival pays a subscription to the Performing Rights Society and advises them of every piece of music to be performed. Individual competitors do not need to obtain copyright for any of their chosen music.

---

[1] British and International Federation of Festivals
[2] Aged 12 and over - 78%

Exercise 2.8

WATERSPORT SAFETY

Windsurfing can be safely enjoyed by almost anyone, by following a few basic guidelines.

1   Learn to windsurf at a recognised centre

2   Wear suitable clothing and beware of the cold

3   Always wear a buoyancy aid and harness

4   Maintain your equipment

5   Follow local advice regarding tides and winds

6   Practice emergency procedures

7   Never sail alone

Correct Training

As well as learning the skill and techniques involved, you need to be taught basic principles about self-rescue and precautions to take with equipment. A recognised centre that is registered with the Royal Yachting Association will ensure you are properly trained.

Clothing

Activity in water causes rapid loss of body heat leading to hypothermia, weakness and delayed reactions. In summer a wet or dry suit 3 mm thick is the minimum requirement. In winter it should have a thickness of 5 mm or more. Be aware of possible heat loss, especially if the winds are blowing from the north or east. Most heat is lost from the

Exercise 2.8 (cont)

2

head, hands and feet and therefore in cold weather a hat[1], gloves and boots are advisable. Woolly hats are not recommended.

Personal Aids

Although a wetsuit will provide some buoyancy, it is advisable to wear a specially designed aid and harness which do not impede your movements. As you progress to wave jumping or speed sailing, a crash helmet will be required.

Equipment

It is vital to ensure that all parts of your board and rig are in good order. Pay particular attention to mast, boom, universal joints and connections, ropes, pulleys, and safety leashes. Rinse metal parts in fresh water at the end of each session.

Weather

Listen to the weather forecast and take advice from the local coastguards, windsurfing shops or sailors about currents and suitable beaches. Never windsurf in fog or at night.

A wind blowing away from the shore is deceptive and dangerous. Choose a beach where the wind blows parallel to the coast, or slightly towards the shore. **NEVER SAIL IN AN OFFSHORE WIND.**

The safest time is at the turn of the tide. Avoid sailing 3 or 4 hours after high or low tide, when the speed of the water flow is at its fastest.

Emergency Procedures

Be prepared for the worst and always carry an orange smoke signal or red distress flare strapped to your wetsuit. Attract attention immediately. Another recognised signal is

---

[1] A tight-fitting neoprene hat is the best.

Exercise 2.8 (cont)

3

slowly raised and lowered outstretched arms. Never leave your board, as it will help to keep you afloat.

If you are experienced and confident, attempt self-rescue[2]. Alternatively, keep warm and paddle to maintain your position. Once you are safely back on the beach, inform the coastguard.

<u>Use the 'Buddy' System</u>

Do not be tempted to sail alone - always go out with a 'buddy'. Make sure that your expected time of return is known by someone ashore and that they keep visual contact with you on the water. If possible, choose a beach with rescue cover. Clubs will provide a friendly means of practising your sport.

---

[2] Techniques taught by the RYA.

Exercise 2.9

THE POND PEOPLE

<u>What We Offer</u>

We specialise in creating features that are designed to enhance your garden as well as attract wildlife. We are an expanding firm of dedicated ecologists offering the following services.

1.   Pond design and construction with adjacent hard and soft landscaping

2.   Pump and filter installation, with associated electrical work

3.   Hard landscaping - paving, patios and paths

4.   Consultancy work on existing ponds and environments

5.   Cleaning repairs and re-stocking

6.   Wildlife garden design, construction and planting

7.   Maintenance service on all the above

<u>More About Us</u>

Our company biologists conduct original research into freshwater environments and ecological systems. They are recognised experts in their particular fields. Our installation teams are staffed by experienced builders and electricians.[*]

We have been established for 15 years and have worked for the private, commercial and public sectors on large and small projects. We arrange lectures and act as consultants for organisations. We work with conservation groups, schools, businesses and clubs.

---

[*] Members of Federation of Master Builders

Exercise 2.9 (cont)

2

<u>Water Works</u>

We will advise you of the optimum shape and depth for the size you require, and where to site it.

The key to a successful pond is careful planting. We will suggest a plant list of specific types and numbers to suit your particular water feature and attract wildlife.

On a summer's day a well-balanced pond can be a fascinating sight: dragonflies darting around the margins, pond skaters skimming the surface, frogs leaping in and out of the water. Birds will enjoy drinking and bathing in the shallows.

<u>Wild Ways</u>

Wildlife gardening is based on the concept that the most likely way of attracting birds, insects and animals into your garden is by using native plants.

In our planting we take into account the conditions prevailing in a particular area and use plants that would occur in similar places in the wild.

A bird shrubbery, butterfly border, wild flower meadow and mixed hedgerows are habitats that can be created in all but the smallest gardens.

<u>Why Choose Us?</u>

We are dedicated to nature conservation and caring for the environment. We offer a rare combination of practical expertise and scientific knowledge.[**]

[**] Six staff members hold science degrees

Exercise 2.9 (cont)

3

As a member of The Guild of Master Craftsmen, our firm takes great pride in its work and can guarantee that you will be satisfied and pleased with the results.

Contact us on 01737 346394 and let us improve your environment.

Exercise 3.1

MONEY BAGS PLC

Money Bags plc is an Independent Financial Adviser, committed to offering straightforward, unbiased advice.

Our company offers its services specifically to people over the age of 50.

Economic Climate

The current situation, with unpredictable stock markets and low interest rates on savings, makes investing difficult.

We aim to help our clients arrange their finances in order to reduce reliance upon any one factor, thus reducing risks and improving yields.

Consultants

All of our advisers have experience with reputable financial institutions They receive regular training and assessment to ensure they maintain our high standards.

Our consultants are assessed on the quality of their recommendations and the standard of service they provide, based on feedback from clients they have advised.

Forward Planning   1

Exercise 3.1 (cont)

MONEY BAGS PLC

<u>Advice</u>

If you need financial advice, one of our consultants can help you to decide

on a course of action, taking into account your complete circumstances,

requirements and objectives.

We offer a wide range of services to clients, covering such matters as

annuities
assurances
bonds
income protection
inheritance tax
investment trusts
pension planning
savings accounts
unit trusts

Forward Planning   2

Exercise 3.1 (cont)

MONEY BAGS PLC

If you have a lump sum to invest or existing investments you wish to review, we can help you to achieve income or growth, or a combination of both.

If you are due to retire in the near future, we can show you how to maximise your income through careful investing.

You may decide to make provision for the costs of long term care. We can help you to plan for the potential burden of residential or nursing care.

Money Bags plc is an Independent Financial Adviser, committed to offering straightforward, unbiased advice.

Forward Planning   3

Exercise 3.2

CAREER MANAGEMENT

Our main purpose is to give independent guidance and information on careers. We also provide a job placing service for younger people leaving education and for those already in the labour market.

<u>Guidance</u>

We help our clients to identify their aims, understand the opportunities open to them and recognise the possibilities of lifelong learning and training. Many of our objectives are achieved through liaising with other organisations such as

District councils

Employers' organisations

Employment groups

Learning and skills councils

Schools and colleges

Support agencies

Voluntary organisations

Young People   1

Exercise 3.2 (cont)

CAREER MANAGEMENT

Education

Advisers work in schools and colleges to offer individual interviews, group work and drop-in sessions.

Consultants will attend parent and open evenings and provide leaflets and software for students and parents. Training and support is also offered to teachers and tutors. Advice is offered to those who may need to adjust their plans in the light of exam results.

Labour Market

Those already in employment can drop into one of the centres or,

if they prefer, phone or e-mail for an appointment.

We have lending libraries of software packages on personal

development and career information in all of our local centres.

Support

Aptitude and skill testing is offered to help people identify their

personal strengths and weaknesses.

Help with CVs, letters of application and interview technique is

given.

We give advice on career routes, current job and training

vacancies and information about trends in the market that are

likely to affect employment.

Young People   2

Exercise 3.2 (cont)

CAREER MANAGEMENT

<u>Employers</u>

We advise employers about opportunities in training and the labour market situation locally. Our expertise is available to help match young people to vacancies.

The assistance we give employers includes displaying job advertisements in our centres and sending flyers out to interested parties.

<u>Other Services</u>

Working within the spheres of education and employment, we are uniquely qualified to offer an insight into what happens to people when they leave full time education. We are well informed about trends in the market and about new government initiatives, together with changes in qualifications and training routes. We are therefore able to offer statistics and guidance on all such matters.

Our main purpose is to give independent guidance and information on careers. We also provide a job placing service for younger people leaving education and for those already in the labour market.

Young People   3

Exercise 3.3

WASTE WATCH

NOT IN MY BACKYARD!

<u>Our Mission</u>

This agency has been set up to provide easy access for the public to information about industrial pollution locally and nationally.

It helps to regulate industry and aids the government in its obligations and commitments.

<u>Emissions</u>

Our pollution inventory contains details of chemical and radioactive emissions from industrial sites nationwide in the following sectors:

Chemical production

Fuel and power production

Manufactured white goods

Material manufacture

Metal production

Mineral processes

Sewage treatment

Waste disposal

People Power   1

Exercise 3.3 (cont)

WASTE WATCH

Data from landfill sites, waste transfer stations and treatment plants was added to the inventory in January 2003.

Smaller scale activities, such as incineration and spraying, are regulated by local authorities.

Other sectors, such as intensive agriculture and food and drink, must report to the agency within the next 5 years.

Collecting Data

The operators of industrial sites are responsible for reporting emissions

of each substance per year.   This must include both planned and

accidental releases, although data is only needed for those that exceed

a set threshold level.

People Power   2

Exercise 3.3 (cont)

WASTE WATCH

Accessing Data

To access the inventory, click on www.pollagent.gov.uk. Information for a particular area can be found through data maps or by keying in a postcode, place name or grid reference.

You can also search using criteria such as name of operator, year of interest, type of process and substances released.

Statistics, including a breakdown of figures, are available from 1999 onwards showing discharges from outlets such as discharge pipes, vents, chimneys, leaks and spillages.

People Power   3

Exercise 3.3 (cont)

WASTE WATCH

<u>Future</u>

This agency has been set up to provide easy access for the public to information about industrial pollution locally and nationally.

Our role will expand over the next few years. European legislation requires us to implement new regulations to cover a wide range of activities including landfills, intensive agriculture and the food and drink industries.

What is in our backyard concerns us all!

People Power   4

Exercise 3.4

PASSPORT PROTOCOL

To travel abroad you should hold a passport that is valid for at least 6 months. Make sure you apply in plenty of time. You may also need a visa to enter certain countries outside the European Union.

Your passport is an important means of identification. Both your identity and the document are open to misuse should it be lost or stolen. Make sure that it is kept in a secure place at all times. When travelling abroad, place it in a hotel safe whenever possible.

YOU MUST REPORT THE LOSS OR THEFT OF YOUR PASSPORT WITHOUT DELAY TO THE POLICE AND THE UKPS, OR, IF YOU ARE ABROAD, TO THE BRITISH CONSULATE, EMBASSY OR HIGH COMMISSION.

To reduce the possibility of misuse, you will be required to complete and sign a declaration form. This is available from your local police station or post office, or by ringing the advice line on 0870 521 0410.

Upon receiving formal notification of loss, the computer data relating to your document is flagged as cancelled. It cannot be reinstated even if your passport subsequently turns up. In this case you should return the document to the UKPS, to ensure its permanent removal from circulation.

To avoid delaying your future travel plans, you should apply for a replacement document as soon as you discover your loss.

Make a note of your passport number and date of issue and ensure you complete the next of kin details inside. Before going abroad, leave a copy of these details with a friend or relative at home and take a second means of photographic identification with you.

Exercise 3.5

SAILING BARGE CHARTER

Charter one of our Thames sailing barges for a day out with a difference.

You can take a trip up the River Swale and enjoy watching the seals sun themselves on the estuary sandbanks.

Alternatively, you may prefer to cruise around the North Kent coast, spotting familiar landmarks and visiting the forts that were built as sea defences during the second world war.

Our barges carry a crew of 4: the skipper, mate and 2 seamen. We only take small groups and require 10-15 people for a day's charter.

You are welcome to bring your own food and drink. Refrigeration is installed, so you can cool your beer or wine. Galley facilities are available, but most of our passengers prefer to bring a picnic so that they can concentrate on the sailing rather than the cooking!

We can organise lunch for you, if you wish. This would consist of a picnic hamper made up especially for your party and supplied by a local caterer.

Before departure we serve hot soup and rolls, coffee and cakes and brief you about the barge and its safety regulations.

We use our engine to move from our mooring, but once underway, the sails are set, the engine cut and peace and calm descends.

We can anchor at interesting locations for lunch, or you can eat underway. If you fancy trying your hand at hauling in the sails or winding the anchor or leeboards, the skipper will welcome your help. However, there is no obligation to participate and you may prefer to sit back, drink and doze and let the scenery slip by you.

Why not give us a ring on 01795 678419 for further details? We shall be delighted to show you around a barge and below decks before you make a booking.

Exercise 3.6

EN-ABLE

En-Able offers a range of computer-based courses that will help you to improve your career prospects.

Whether you want to brush up your skills before returning to work, prepare for promotion or for a move to a new job, we have the package for you.

Our database covers most areas of employment and recognised qualifications. You can choose your style from self or tutor aided and full or part time study.

The following list shows just a few options from the wide range of modular courses we offer.

Business studies
Childcare
Complementary therapies
Computing
Counselling
English
Languages
Mathematics
Sport and leisure
Teaching

Words and Numbers - a FREE course to improve literacy and numeracy skills for those whose native language is English. There is an alternative FREE course offered to help foreign speakers to improve their knowledge of English.

We have more than 1,500 centres throughout Great Britain. They are located in libraries, community and sports centres and in the high streets of major towns. You can even work from home, as long as you have access to the Internet.

Our courses are uniquely flexible and recognise your individual needs. They enable you to study at your own pace and in local venues within the community.

For free advice, call us on 0800 198 276 from 0800 hrs - 2200 hrs, 7 days a week.

We will discuss the various options with you and help you to choose the path that is best suited to your requirements.

Exercise 3.7

MEMORANDUM

FROM   Lucy Rose

TO   Dillon Jacks

REF   LR/Staff/73

DATE   (date of exercise)

We talked about doing something different for our team outing this coming summer.

I have received a flyer from a local firm that offers Thames sailing barges for charter, and think this might appeal to everyone.

We could hire a barge for the day and take a trip up the River Swale, embarking and disembarking in Whitstable harbour, and then book an early evening meal at the "Lobster Quadrille" on the quayside.

To keep costs down, Usama could be asked to provide drinks and a cold buffet lunch for us to eat onboard.

If you think this is worth looking into, the barge company would be happy to show us around one of their vessels before we make a booking. We can ring them on 01795 678419 for further details.

Copy: Usama Hussain
       File

(You should have printed 2 extra copies, indicating the routing on each)

Exercise 3.8

Zenith Bank Ltd 109 Caber Street GLASGOW G68 0VW

(date of exercise)

Our ref GS/NB/728196

Mr Fin Witag
8 High Street
KINGUSSIE
PH21 1HX

Dear Mr Witag

There has never been a better time to apply for the Zenith Gold Card.

If you apply for your card before 1st April you will pay no interest on all purchases and balance transfers for the first 6 months.

After that, we offer a low long term rate of just 13.5% (APR variable) on all purchases. You can take advantage of interest free credit for up to 55 days if you clear your balance in full every month. Alternatively you can make a monthly payment of 2% of the outstanding balance.

There is no annual fee to pay and you can transfer all of your existing store and credit card balances to our Gold Card, thus saving yourself time and money. With a credit limit tailored to your requirements, you will benefit from increased spending power whenever you need it.

To take advantage of these benefits, simply complete the enclosed application form and return it to us without delay.

You have a number of rights under the Consumer Credit Act. You have a right to settle this Agreement at any time by giving notice in writing and paying off all amounts payable under the Agreement. If you have obtained unsatisfactory goods or services under a transaction financed by this Agreement, apart from any purchased out of a cash loan, you may have a right to sue the supplier or us.

We look forward to being of service to you.

Yours sincerely

Guo Lishan
Marketing

Enc

Copy: Mark Goodyer, File *(You should have printed 2 extra copies, indicating the routing on each)*

Exercise 3.9

WELLWISE *HORUS BUSINESS PARK   EASTLEIGH   HAMPSHIRE SO53 8TY*

(date of exercise)

Our ref GPH/Client.875234

Mrs Olga Djokanovic
34 Hill Green
LAVENHAM
Suffolk CO10 5FG

Dear Mrs Djokanovic

As one of our healthcare policyholders, you will have received issues of our quarterly magazine. However, this is a very special edition of Wellwise, which marks the launch of a new service for our individual private medical insurance customers.

It is an online service called Health Watch and it is available only through the Internet. It is aimed at helping you and your family maintain your health and is an extension of our existing helpline telephone service.

In this issue of Wellwise, we explain exactly how Health Watch works. We describe in detail the structure and medical expertise behind the setting up of the service. You will discover how the symptom synopsis, medical dictionary, helpline and planner can give you confidence and reassurance.

To access Health Watch visit www.HealthWatch.co.uk, select <u>New User</u> and enter your personal code: HW6752D56pmi and complete the registration form.

Wellwise also has fascinating articles about such wide ranging subjects as claims made for various popular diets to the arguments about immunising young children. There is an amusing commentary about the use of red wine versus white wine, for medicinal purposes only, of course!

Visit us at Health Watch today and enjoy the peace of mind that our professional expertise can bring to your home.

Yours sincerely

Clem Burke
Manager

Copy: Alex Blackman
        File

(You should have printed 2 extra copies, indicating the routing on each)

Exercise 3.10

ZENITH BANK PLC

DEPOSIT	WITHDRAWAL	INTEREST
Cash	Available immediately	Commences from next working day
Cheque deposited to account with cash card only	Available after 5 working days	Commences after 3 working days
Automated credits	Available immediately	Commences from next working day

FEES AND CHARGES

TYPE	INTEREST EAR %	MONTHLY RATE %	FEE £
Agreed overdraft	6.75	0.55	-
Unauthorised overdraft	19.09	1.52	12.00
Unpaid items due to insufficient funds	-	-	27.50 per item
Special clearance for cheques	-	-	15.00 per item
Deposit of foreign currency cheque	-	-	5.00 per item

Exercise 3.11

SPRING SATURDAY SPECIALS 2004

COURSES ON CAMPUS

CODE	SUBJECT	DATE AND TIME	FEE £
SS1	Violent times - domestic and international politics	10 April, 1000 - 1600 hrs	15.75
SS2	Digital photography workshop	17 April, 1000 - 1630 hrs	25.00, covers materials
SS3	Architecture from Baroque to Palladian	8 May, 1000 - 1600 hrs	15.75
SS4	Present your facts with PowerPoint	15 May, 1100 - 1600 hrs	20.50, covers floppy disk and handouts
SS5	History of British wines	22 May, 1800 - 2130 hrs	30.00, includes buffet and wine tasting

COURSES OFF CAMPUS

VENUE	CODE	SUBJECT	DATE	TIME	FEE £
The Pinetum	SSV1	Identifying birdsong	3 April	0700 - 1000 hrs	9.50
Black Friars' Abbey	SSV2	Black Friars' dig revisited	8 May	1100 - 1530 hrs	15.00
North Reach Docks	SSV3	Maritime history	15 May	1000 - 1600 hrs	18.50

Exercise 3.12

ARTS FESTIVAL

GROUP MIME

TYPE	CLASS	AGE	TIME (MINS)	FEE £	NOTE
Groups comprised of at least 2 members and no more than 4 members	109	11 years and under	4	8.50	In all mime classes music and limited costumes and props may be used. Check detailed rules with organisers beforehand.
	110	12-14 years	4	9.00	
	111	15-17 years	4	9.00	
Groups comprised of at least 5 members and no more than 15 members	112	11 years and under	8	15.00	
	113	12-14 years	8	15.00	
	114	15-17 years	10	17.50	

CHORAL VERSE SPEAKING

CLASS	AGE	TIME (MINS)	FEE £	DESCRIPTION
225	11 years and under	5	9.00	Comprising any poem or rhyme, spoken as a group, with limited actions. No music, costumes or props allowed.
226	12-14 years	5	10.50	

Text production practice exam 1 – Document 1

Country House Trust   577 Earlham Road   NORWICH   NR4 7HW
Tel/Fax - (01603) 459768   enquiries@chtrust.org.uk   www.chtrust.org.uk

(date of exercise)

Our ref   GRM24/288

Your ref   FY/SK/Social

Mrs S Youel
Focus Youth Group
280 London Road
KING'S LYNN
Norfolk   PE34 6RY

Dear Mrs Youel

GROUP MEMBERSHIP

Welcome to the Country House Trust. We are delighted that you have decided to join our group scheme. As requested, we have pleasure in enclosing the 12 membership cards for you to distribute to your branches. **We would remind you that, to obtain free access to our properties, it is necessary for the group leader to produce a valid card at the start of any visit.**

Thank you for giving us permission to reclaim tax on any subscriptions or donations you make to the trust. Additional funds generated by this scheme are greatly appreciated by us. The extra income enables us to extend our conservation work even further.

The booklets in the enclosed welcome packs give information on the properties that belong to our trust. There is a programme of events, including concerts, lectures and guided walks. There is also a full educational programme that gives students an opportunity for research, historical role-play and many other enjoyable activities. We note your wish to be involved in such activities.

We hope that your organisation will gain great benefit and enjoyment from your membership during the coming year.

We shall contact you shortly to arrange the proposed meeting.

Yours sincerely

Alex Gray
Customer Care Manager

Encs

Text production practice exam 1 – Document 2

MEMO

From Alex Gray

To Marcia Dobson

Ref AG/GRM24/288

Date (date of exercise)

URGENT

I am attaching a copy of the correspondence I have been exchanging with Mrs Youel. She is the Focus Youth Group's secretary and is likely to be a very useful contact. Her experience with young people could prove helpful when we develop the historical role-play exercises planned for next season. Please contact her without delay to arrange a meeting to discuss her members' possible involvement in such activities. I should also like to be there and could make a lunchtime appointment on any day during the week starting Monday *(you should have inserted here the date for the first Monday of next month)*.

Can you give me a progress report on the restoration work being undertaken at Holly Hatch House? Last time I enquired, the Lyttleton Suite in the east quarter was being refurbished. I am hoping that it is now complete, as this accommodation, together with the servants' rooms on the top floor, is planned to be used for educational activities.

We shall also need to check that the health and safety regulations we already have in place will cover the change of use. Please ask Angus to take responsibility for this. The reason why I am keen to get any such problems sorted out now is to avoid any difficulties such as we have had in the past.

Enc

Text production practice exam 1 – Document 3

HOLLY HATCH MANOR

RECENT DEVELOPMENTS

One of our recent acquisitions, this 17th century manor is undergoing renovation, which will take approximately 5 years to complete. However, we are now about to open the house to the public. Some parts of the building will be subject to temporary closure, but we guarantee you will still find your visit worthwhile.

You will have the chance to see some of the restoration work being carried out. Much of the repairs to curtains, furniture and fabrics will be carried out on site. The original foundry and workshops are able to deal with most of the metal and woodwork repairs. The Lyttleton Suite in the east quarter is being refurbished and will form part of the accommodation to be utilised for educational activities.

<u>Programme of Work</u>

Although most of the structural work is now complete, we are about to embark upon phase 2, which is as follows

1   Cleaning silverware

2   Restoring and cleaning china

3   Cleaning and repair of fabrics and wall/hangings

4   Setting up new displays throughout the rooms

5   Equipping the education block

6   Completing the new restaurant

Text production practice exam 1 – Document 3 (cont)

2

<u>Educational Programme</u>

We plan an exciting range of activities for groups from youth and adult clubs, schools

and colleges. They will have the chance to take part in historical role-play based on the

daily lives of household servants, from the butler to the lowly scullery maid. Courses

will be held on furniture, fabric, glass and china renovation. A series of lecture lunches

will cover topics as varied as bricks and mortar, 17th century cooking and Tudor

England[1]. Many of the original archives of the house will be made available for studying

on site. Copies of key historical documents and <u>interactive computer programs relating</u>

<u>to the era</u> will also be set up for students.

<u>Barn Restaurant</u>

Our luxurious licensed restaurant, which is due to open in October, is situated behind the
main house in a restored hammer-beam barn. With its exposed beams, it provides a
magnificent setting for our haute cuisine[2]. You can be confident that we shall live up to
these claims for our cooking.

We aim to use local produce, including vegetables, salads and herbs from our kitchen
garden. The menu will be changed according to the season.

For the first fortnight we shall open daily at lunchtime only. After that, we shall also be
open for evening meals, apart from Sundays.

Morning and afternoon snacks will be served in the sun room and the loggia. Details

regarding menus, prices and times will be sent to you shortly, or you can ring us on

01263 897009.

---

[1] A social history of the times
[2] Cookery of a very high standard

Text production practice exam 1 – Document 3 (cont)

3

<u>Gardens and Estate</u>

Work began early on the gardens nearest the house. The walled vegetable beds are already productive, although the glasshouses all need attention. The pineapple pit will need to be restored by specialists in the longer term.

The formal lawns surrounded with clipped hedges and topiary yew trees have been restored to their former glory. Most of the herbaceous borders have been rescued from the undergrowth and replanted ready for the coming season. The more modern rock garden with its water features and alpine plants is also in full working order.

Some of the outlying parts of the estate are still suffering from neglect. Plans are in hand to thin and tidy the coppices. Many of the boundary fences need replacing. One ambitious project is to restore the lake area and repair the fountain and waterfall, but this long term scheme will have to wait until phase 4.

The estate includes a working farm that boasts a large herd of Guernsey cows. As well as producing milk, cream and cheese, the farm provides the estate with its own free-range chickens and eggs. All these products will be used in the new restaurant.

Text production practice exam 2 – Document 1

Beaumont (Vintners) PLC Castle Rise WINDSOR Berkshire SL4 8YT
Telephone 01753 865093   Fax 01753 865100

(date of exercise)

Our ref MS/Prom.269

Your ref NMcC/PP

PERSONAL

Mr N McCrathie
Forrester & Son
203 Lever Street
BRACKNELL
Berks RG12 6PQ

Dear Mr McCrathie

CHAMPAGNE TREAT

Next month we are holding a special wine tasting evening to promote an interesting range
of champagnes.

In appreciation of your loyalty and the long association of our companies, we have
pleasure in inviting you to the event.   Enclosed are 4 tickets for your personal use and the
use of your colleagues.

The tasting starts at 2000 hrs and will be directed by the head of our buying
department, Claudette Simone. A hot and cold finger buffet will be available throughout
the evening. Prior to the tasting a short video, Champagne: From Grape to Glass, will be
shown. This features Rheims and Epernay vineyards and the process the grapes undergo
to transform them into a quality product.

You may wish to take the opportunity to order cases of the various champagnes featured
during the event. **They will be offered, at very attractive bargain prices, only to those
attending this occasion.**

We do hope that you will be able to attend what we are sure will prove to be a successful
and enjoyable evening.

Yours sincerely

Marius Shaw
Promotions Manager

Encs

Text production practice exam 2 – Document 2

MEMORANDUM

TO Cass Martin

FROM Marius Shaw

REF MS/Prom.270

DATE (date of exercise)

I trust the arrangements for next month's wine tasting are well in hand.

Please make sure that the Highlander Hotel, which has not always been reliable in the past, provides us with a suitable room in which to show the video Champagne: From Grape to Glass. The room should be close to the conference hall and seat up to 200 people.

Claudette Simone, who is directing the tasting, has asked for the main hall to be laid out with round tables each seating 10. A long table is to be provided on the dais. It might be politic to contact Claudette's secretary to see whether she has any other special requirements.

I am attaching a draft article with information that our guests may find interesting. Please send a fair copy of this to the printers without delay. They guarantee to include it in the tasting catalogue as long as they receive it by Friday *(you should have inserted here the date for the first Friday of next month)*. I think it will provide a useful introduction to the proceedings if inserted before the listings and tasting notes.

Please keep me informed of any problems that may arise. I am out of the office for the remainder of the week but should like to meet up with you on my return to discuss developments and finalise the arrangements.

Att

Text production practice exam 2 – Document 3

THE BEST BUBBLY

True champagne can come only from a strictly demarcated region in northern France. It is made in the traditional way and manufacturers are subject to very rigid controls.

Styles are based on the variety of grape used. The dry, non-vintage champagnes are usually a blend of black and white grapes, whilst the vintage wine is made from one variety and in smaller amounts.

Producers

Most of the vines are cultivated by local farmers, often on a part-time basis, who sell their grapes to the big houses or to co-operatives. Some even make wine themselves or buy it back, once it has been processed, to label and sell as their own. This means that there is no limit to the number of brands on the market. However, there are approximately 20 houses with the best-known names and the widest distribution. Their size and wealth allows them to use expensive equipment, employ the most experienced staff and store their vintage as long as possible. Their products thus become the brand leaders.

Method

Harvesting takes place, with great care to avoid breaking whole grapes and with split fruit rejected, as prematurely crushed grapes give colour to the juice. If necessary the crop is sorted by hand before passing into huge vertical presses, which hold 4 tons each. The pressing is repeated 3 or 4 times with the cake of skins and stalks being divided and redistributed each time. The first pressing is kept for the house blend and the remaining

Text production practice exam 2 – Document 3 (cont)

2

must is left to ferment[*]. If it is too acidic it is decanted into steel tanks that encourage a

secondary fermentation.

The wine is racked several times during the winter months to cleanse it. In the spring it is

tasted and sorted into lots for blending. It is then bottled and precise measures of yeast

and sugar are added. This causes fermentation to begin again to produce the fizz.

Storage

The wine is stored in cold, dark, limestone cellars for between 2 and 5 years, depending
on the vintage.

After several months the bottles are moved to special racks that enable them to be slightly
shaken, twisted and tipped daily[**] until they stand vertically. This results in the yeast
sediment collecting at the end of the cork. The bottles' necks are then passed through a
freezing tank, the corks are removed and the pressure inside blows the frozen sediment
out. The contents are immediately topped up and mushroom corks wired into place.

The bottles are returned to the cellar to rest and be allowed to mature. They are then
washed, labelled and embellished with the distinctive gold foil cover that is the hallmark
of true champagne.

Storing and Serving at Home

Think of champagne as just like any other wine, with styles to suit all types of occasions

and accompany many different kinds of food. Most people cannot tell the difference

between a modestly priced and an expensive vintage.

---

[*] in aged oak barrels
[**] for about 3 months

Text production practice exam 2 – Document 3 (cont)

3

There are a few suggestions for storing and serving:

1   Keep new champagne for at least 3 months

2   Buy a bottle each month, drinking the oldest first

3   Store in a cold place - a cellar or old fridge in a garage

4   Cool for 20 minutes before serving in a bucket of half ice and half cold water

5   Allow 3 glasses per head for a party but only half as much if served as an aperitif or used as a toast

6   Remove the wire, cover the cork with a tea towel and ease off gently

7   To preserve the bubbles, pour slowly into a slightly tilted glass

8   Any trace of grease or detergent on a glass can affect the fizz

This glorious drink should be enjoyed whenever the mood takes you and not reserved just for special occasions.

Word processing practice exam 1 – Document 1

COMMUNITY SAFETY

DOCUMENT 1

HOME ZONE PATROL

Our company is proud to offer you a unique, valuable and reliable service.

ABOUT THE COMPANY

This internationally based company is managed by a team of executives who have gained experience from working in many different areas of the security sector. Our managers have experience of providing services to residential communities throughout Europe. The company was started in Italy 8 years ago.

Each control centre covers a limited number of clients within a defined area. These centres are manned by local personnel who know the neighbourhood and its particular concerns. All such staff are carefully screened and either have police, emergency service or military backgrounds.

INTRODUCTION   1

Word processing practice exam 1 – Document 1 (cont)

COMMUNITY SAFETY

WHAT WE COVER

We offer the following facilities:

first aid help

immediate response to alarms

response to third party calls

school patrols at arrival and departure times

second key holder function

securing damaged property

storage of clients' critical data

vehicle patrols pass properties every hour

EXTRA COVER

For an additional fee we guarantee to carry out a check twice a day of premises where owners are on holiday or on long term postings abroad. Confirmation and duration of survey is logged and supplied to the owners by e-mail. We can mount silent remote control panic alarms to the outside of your property. We also provide a digital and video record of valuables, which can be used to assist insurance claims.

INTRODUCTION   2

Word processing practice exam 1 – Document 1 (cont)

COMMUNITY SAFETY

PATROL SYSTEM

Our vehicles are 4-wheel drive Combotrucks, thus allowing us to cope with all weather conditions. All vehicles are equipped with a full range of emergency equipment, including first aid and fire fighting apparatus.

All personnel have voice and data communication with their bases, including a satellite tracking and monitoring system. There are backup patrols in the event of multiple alarms.

Each vehicle services not more than 300 premises within its residential area. This ensures high quality maintenance and fast response times.

We are proud to offer a supporting role to existing emergency services. Our clients have the peace of mind of knowing that we are able to respond immediately.

INTRODUCTION   3

Word processing practice exam 1 – Document 1 (cont)

COMMUNITY SAFETY

SCREENING AND TRAINING

All our staff are carefully checked through police computer data records. Only those with impeccable references and credentials are accepted for training.

The training of our response personnel is rigorous and they are required to attend refresher courses frequently. In addition to tuition on a wide range of security issues, they receive intensive training in crime scene protection, advanced driving, primary first aid and basic fire fighting.

CHARGES

The standard package is available as a special introductory offer at a cost of under £5 per day. The rates for extra cover can be negotiated based on individual requirements.

Our company is proud to offer you a unique, valuable and reliable service.

INTRODUCTION   4

Word processing practice exam 1 – Document 2

HOME ZONE PATROL 150 Scarcroft Road YORK YO2 4DG
Tel & Fax: 01904 699843   **www.homezone.co.uk**

(date of exercise)

Our ref GV/HZP/Promo

Mr D Arkell
The Grange
Wildernesse Avenue
YORK   YO3 5SJ

Dear Mr Arkell

We are pleased to announce that we have extended our operation to cover the city of York. You may have noticed our patrol vehicles in your locality during the past few weeks. We have been surveying the area prior to offering our service to a select number of clients.

Home Zone Patrol provides a unique emergency response service to client home owners. It ensures that immediate response is available 24 hours a day. Our special introductory offer is a weekly rate of £30 for our standard cover with the rate fixed for a full year.

> Our patrols are manned by fully trained personnel. They drive past each client's home at least once an hour throughout the day and night. They will <u>respond immediately</u> to any alarm, regardless of severity, cause or frequency. Their brief is to provide a front line response to threat or harm caused by criminals, vandals, general disturbances, accidents or natural disasters.

In today's society, in which 1 out of 3 people are victims of crime at some stage in their lives, we aim to bring you and your family peace of mind. Although it is a fairly new concept in this country, the service we offer is a welcome and common facility in Europe and America.

You are one of the select home owners in York to whom we are making our initial approach. If you think that our service will be of benefit to you, we should be delighted to arrange an appointment at our offices or in your home. Just give us a ring at the number on our letterhead. We look forward to helping keep your community, your family and your home secure.

Yours sincerely

Guillio Vincente
Director UK Operations

Copy: Digby Lyttleton, File *(You should have printed 2 extra copies, indicating the routing on each)*

Word processing practice exam 1 – Document 3

FIRE FIGHTING

If a fire breaks out in your home, alert the emergency services and home zone. Our Combotruck patrol vehicles can reach you quickly and carry extinguishers and basic equipment to deal with minor fires. In the meantime, there are some basic actions you should take to help reduce injury and damage.

The most important thing is to get everyone out of the house. When following your escape route, if a door feels hot, do not open it. Close doors and windows behind you, to reduce the spread of flames and fumes. Keep as near to the floor as possible.

If you are above the ground floor, knot bedding or clothing together to form a rope and secure it to heavy furniture. Use this to climb down as far as you can before jumping. If there is no safe way down, shut the door, open the window and shout for help.

Do not attempt to tackle a fire yourself if it is fierce or spreading. When using an extinguisher you should heed the following advice.

Switch off the current if electricity is involved. Ensure the extinguisher is suitable for the fire you are tackling. Aim at the base of the fire, sweeping the nozzle from side to side and working steadily inwards from the edges.

Keep a level head and do not panic. Remember, help is on its way.

In your car you should install a 1.4 kg extinguisher containing either dry powder or vaporising liquid. Keep it secured beneath the dashboard or in the driver's footwell, but not in the boot. Ideally you should have it checked annually.

Word processing practice exam 1 – Document 4

DOCUMENT 4

YORK CONTROL CENTRE - STAFFING

KEY OFFICE BASED PERSONNEL

NAME	JOB TITLE	CONTACT NUMBER	ADDRESS
Guillio Vincente	Director UK Operations	01904 647566	16 Holgate Road, York, YO2 6BN
Ernest Arnold	Centre Manager	01904 639009	33 Scarcroft Lane, York, YO1 9NB
Molly Longley	Control Co-ordinator	01904 622659	20 North Road, Bootham, Y03 6PY
Jack Dillon	Technical Supervisor	01756 793667	Low Farm, Skipton, BD23 7GH
Nadia Porter	Operations Administrator	01751 431268	The Grange, Sinnington, YO6 7RT

PATROL PERSONNEL ROTA - WEEK 1

SECTOR	ROLE	NAME	SHIFT	RATE PER HOUR £
Alpha	Patrol chief	Bernie Miles	Early	18.00
Alpha	Driver	Maggie Henderson	Early	14.50
Beta	Patrol chief	Varun Bhadeshia	Late	18.00
Beta	Driver and first-aider	Denzil Peach	Late	17.25
Charlie	Patrol chief and paramedic	Paula Woods	Night	24.75
Charlie	Driver	Jason Kendall	Night	16.00
All	Standby officer	Miles Trumper	Day (12 hours)	7.50
All	Standby officer	David Levy	Night (12 hours)	9.00

Word processing practice exam 2 – Document 1

DOCUMENT 1

SECURITY

TRAVELLING SAFELY

HINTS FOR DRIVERS AND PASSENGERS

<u>Maintenance and Safety Checks</u>

Study the driver's handbook that is provided with your vehicle. The invaluable information it contains includes a step-by-step guide to the basic checks you should carry out to maintain your car safely.

Preferably each week, but definitely prior to long journeys, check the levels of petrol, engine oil, brake fluid, coolant and windscreen wash. Clean the lights, front and rear windscreens, and ensure washers and wipers are working efficiently. Check all lights, replacing any bulbs that may have blown. Regularly carry out an inspection of the engine pipes, hoses and fluid reservoirs, looking for possible leakage.

Make sure all tyres are kept at the correct pressure and that treads are within the statutory limits. The handbook contains information about the correct pressures for front and rear tyres. It also recommends adjustments for different weather conditions.

Regular servicing by a reputable garage is very important. The vehicle logbook lists the recommended services depending on the age of your car or the mileage.

MODERN MOTORING   1

Word processing practice exam 2 – Document 1 (cont)

SECURITY

<u>Safety Appliances</u>

There are many different brands that fall into the following categories:

adult seatbelt
booster cushion
bucket seat
carrycot harness
carrycot restraint
child harness
dog safety belt
estate car grilles

When buying a child's safety seat, first consider the age of the child. Bear in mind that he or she will grow. Whichever type of seat or harness you buy, make sure it complies with British Standard BS3254 or European Standard ECE44.

<u>Birth to 9 Months</u>

Use a carrycot restraint with straps that secure it to the rear seat. The harness should have a quick release buckle. Alternatively, a first size bucket seat can be fitted on the front or rear passenger seat, with the baby facing towards the rear.

MODERN MOTORING   2

Word processing practice exam 2 – Document 1 (cont)

SECURITY

Between 9 Months and 5 Years

A bucket seat fastened to the rear seat is suitable. Some models are secured with a diagonal seat belt. This makes them easy to adapt to different vehicles. There must be a crotch strap to pass between the child's legs.

Over 5 Years

Either a child's harness or an adult safety belt with a special booster cushion can be used on a back seat.

Protection Against Theft

Only the most sophisticated security systems will deter a professional thief. However, fairly simple ones will put off casual thieves and joy riders. Locking devices for handbrakes, steering-wheels and gear levers are effective.   Another basic deterrent is to etch the windows with the registration number. This would put off a thief, as windows and number plates would need replacing.

Sophisticated electrical systems will either set off an alarm if doors are tampered with or immobilise the ignition system.

MODERN MOTORING   3

Word processing practice exam 2 – Document 1 (cont)

SECURITY

Sophisticated devices include push-button codes, ultrasonic sensors and voltage sensors. Such devices are often fitted as standard in top of the range vehicles, but are increasingly offered as options on moderately priced models.

Regular servicing by a reputable garage is very important. The vehicle logbook lists the recommended services depending on the age of your car or the mileage.

MODERN MOTORING   4

Word processing practice exam 2 – Document 2

DOCUMENT 2

COPING WITH CAR ACCIDENTS

Should you be involved in an accident, you <u>must stop immediately</u> if any person, other than yourself, has been injured. If damage has been caused to another car or property, or a domestic animal, other than a cat, has been injured, you are also obliged to stop. **Failing to do so is an offence involving a fine, endorsement on your licence and possible disqualification.**

You are required to remain long enough to exchange names and addresses with all involved, take registration numbers and establish ownership of vehicles.

If, for example, you hit an empty parked vehicle, you may leave the scene. However, you must report it to the police, in person, within 24 hours.

To avoid more vehicles becoming involved, it is important to warn other traffic. Call the police if anyone is hurt or the road is blocked. Anyone badly hurt should be moved by medically qualified persons only.

ONCE ANY INJURED ARE RECEIVING ATTENTION, TAKE PARTICULARS AND FIND WITNESSES. RECORD ANY EVIDENCE ON THE SPOT, EITHER BY DRAWING A DIAGRAM OR TAKING PHOTOGRAPHS.

The risk of severe injuries to passengers can be reduced by taking sensible precautions. Seat belts should always be fastened. Babies and children should use suitable safety seats and harnesses. Make sure they comply with British Standard BS3254 or European Standard ECE44.

Many new cars come with airbags fitted or offered as optional extras. Although they can work very efficiently to minimise injury, they can be dangerous to babies or young children. For that reason, such passengers should not travel in seats with airbags.

Word processing practice exam 2 – Document 3

DOCUMENT 3

COURSES ON CAR MAINTENANCE AND SAFETY

Title	Content	Venue	Date	Time hrs	Session Fee £
Securing Your Vehicle	Fitting alarms, combination locks, window etching	City Polytechnic	6, 13 Sept	1830	9.75
Basic Maintenance	Checking fluids, tyres, lights, brakes etc	Reigate Polytechnic	4, 11 Dec	1030	9.75
Advanced Maintenance	Adjusting fan belt, flushing radiator, repairing dents	Reigate Polytechnic	13, 20 Oct	1900	15.50
Holiday Travelling	Towing, legal documents and requirements abroad, driving in snow, car hire, insurance	Mattheson's Travel plc, Redhill	20, 27 Nov	1000	17.00

COPING WITH ACCIDENTS

Content	Details	Date and Time
Responding to the incident, first aid, recording details, legal responsibilities and implications, insurance matters.	Two one-day courses at the City Polytechnic, designed to help you deal with traffic accidents confidently and efficiently. The auto repair yard will be used to stage incidents. Theory will be taught in the adjoining classroom.	9 and 23 October from 1000 hrs to 1600 hrs

Word processing practice exam 2 – Document 4

DOCUMENT 4

Reigate Polytechnic   London Road   REIGATE   RH2 7JD
Tel & Fax 01737 665578

(date of exercise)

Our ref CMCourses/HT2/35

Mrs P Dawson
68 Merstham Road
REDHILL   RH1 4DC

Dear Mrs Dawson

I refer to your telephone call last month when you enquired about the short courses we were starting in the autumn on vehicle maintenance and safety. You were interested to know whether we were able to offer a course covering holiday travel. I understand that you and your family plan to drive across France to southern Spain, towing a caravan for the first time.

Our marketing team discovered that there was interest in such a course and that a local travel agent would be happy to sponsor and host two sessions. These will be held at Mattheson's Travel plc in Redhill on 20 and 27 November from 1000 hrs to 1600 hrs. Their staff training facilities can accommodate up to 20 delegates and their catering manager will provide morning coffee, a cold buffet lunch and afternoon tea and cake for each session for an additional charge of £10 per head.

> You may also find that another course we are running in October would be of use to you. This gives practical advice about how to cope with accidents in this country and abroad. It helps you to ensure that your insurance arrangements are adequate. In view of the fact that this is your first journey abroad, towing your caravan, such a course would provide you with valuable information and help boost your confidence.

I am unable to let you know the fee for this course, as I am awaiting this information from the City Polytechnic, where the sessions will be held. These have proved extremely popular in the past. As soon as I have any further details I will contact you, so that you can make an early application, should you be interested.

Yours sincerely

Nick Parsons
Administrative Officer

Copy: Jim Tomlinson, File   *(You should have printed 2 extra copies, indicating the routing on each)*

Section 6

Letterheads and memo headings

This section provides printed header paper for your use in all the exercises and practice exams in Sections 1–4. They are for you to use, should you prefer to print onto headed paper.

These headings are also available on the CD-ROM, should you prefer to recall the templates into your files.

CENTURY BANKING PLC 140 George St EDINBURGH EH2 5PW
www.centurybank.com

FitFun 273 Victoria Street LONDON SW1E 3MP
Tel/Fax 020 7730 2689 E-mail services@fitfun.com

Bingham-Newland Travel

80 Milton Road PETERBOROUGH PE6 4SD

Tel: 0733 380653   www.bing-new.com   travel@bing-new.co.uk

MEMORANDUM

FROM

TO

REF

DATE

Memorandum

From

To

Ref

Date

Bingham-Newland Travel

MEMO

To

From

Ref

Date

MEMORANDUM

FROM

TO

REF

DATE

Zenith Bank Ltd 109 Caber Street GLASGOW G68 0VW

Country House Trust   577 Earlham Road   NORWICH   NR4 7HW
Tel/Fax - (01603) 459768   enquiries@chtrust.org.uk   www.chtrust.org.uk

MEMO

From

To

Ref

Date

Beaumont (Vintners) PLC   Castle Rise   WINDSOR   Berkshire   SL4 8YT
Telephone 01753 865093   Fax 01753 865100

MEMORANDUM

TO

FROM

REF

DATE

HOME ZONE PATROL 150 Scarcroft Road YORK YO2 4DG
Tel & Fax: 01904 699843   www.homezone.co.uk

ST NO	£15.99
ACC NO	051933
	652.5
	12.10.04
	D.W.J

Reigate Polytechnic   London Road   REIGATE   RH2 7JD
Tel & Fax 01737 665578

S 999 OFF 08

Let the web do the work!

Why not visit our website and see what it can do for you?

Free online support materials

You can download free support materials for many of our Office Technology products. We even offer a special e-alert service to notify you when new content is posted.

Lists of useful weblinks

Our site includes lists of other websites, which can save you hours of research time.

Online ordering – 24 hours a day

It's quick and simple to order your resources online, and you can do it anytime – day or night!

Find your consultant

The website helps you find your nearest Heinemann consultant, who will be able to discuss your needs and help you find the most cost-effective way to buy.

It's time to save time – visit our website now!

www.heinemann.co.uk/vocational

t 01865 888068   **f** 01865 314029   **e** orders@heinemann.co.uk   **w** www.heinemann.co.uk

Heinemann
Inspiring generations

J492